Dominic Bradbury **NEW COUNTRY HOUSES**

Dominic Bradbury **NEW COUNTRY HOUSES**

Abbeville Press Publishers
New York London

First published in the United States of America
in 2005 by Abbeville Press,
137 Varick Street, 5th Floor, New York, NY 10013

First published in Great Britain in 2005 by
Laurence King Publishing Ltd,
71 Great Russell Street, London WC1B 3BP

Library of Congress Cataloging-in-Publication Data
Bradbury, Dominic.
New country houses / Dominic Bradbury.
      p. cm.
Includes bibliographical references and index.
ISBN 0-7892-0851-2 (hc)
ISBN 0-7892-0853-9 (pbk)
(alk. paper)
 1. Country homes. 2. Architecture, Domestic.
3. Architecture, Modern—20th century.
4. Architecture, Modern—21st century. I. Title.
   NA7600.B73 2005
   728'.37'09173409049—dc22
                         2004023395

Printed in China

Project managed by Anne McDowall
Designed by John Round Design
Picture research by Claire Gouldstone

To Florence, Cecily and Noah,
who love the country life.

ACKNOWLEDGEMENTS
With thanks to Zoe Antoniou, Faith Bradbury,
Philip Cooper, Liz Faber, Claire Gouldstone,
Anne McDowall, Jonny Pegg & Curtis Brown,
John Round and all at Laurence King. And thanks
also to all of the architects – and their clients – who
have assisted in the development of this book.

Jacket illustration
Mountain Guest House, Mack Scogin Merril Elam,
Dillard, Georgia, USA (photographer: Timothy Hursley)

Previous page: Büchel House

CONTENTS

NEW COUNTRY HOUSE
INTRODUCTION

The country house carries a heavy load of symbolic weight and historical connotation. From the sprawling, classical country house to the more modest, Modernist-inspired escape, class and cultural markers garland, and sometimes tarnish, the popular idea of the bucolic retreat. The more progressive of these associations carry the country house forward, confirming its continued place in the architectural and cultural order, whereas the negative views firmly pull the country house back into the pages of history and seek to keep it a relic of the past. But in fact, there is no stopping the continuing evolution of the country house as it begins to move into a new era, an era of renewed focus upon the countryside itself and the way in which we choose to live a particular kind of rural life. The new country house is a vibrant response to a revitalised passion for countryside living and the search for homes which truly reflect the desires, aspirations and lifestyle of an increasingly design-conscious group of contemporary disciples following the gospel of the pastoral and the provincial.

this page Sir John Vanbrugh's baroque plans for Blenheim Palace, Oxfordshire, UK, were still not fully realized at the time of the death of his client, the Duke of Marlborough, in 1722.

near right Henry David Thoreau's cabin at Walden Pond, Massachusetts – the original "house in the woods".

far right Ludwig Mies van der Rohe's Farnsworth House (1950), in Plano, Illinois. Raised on stilts, this elegant glass box floating in a field is one of the most influential Modernist houses.

THE CONTEXT

The country house has always embodied a complex set of messages tied to ideas of status, class, wealth and the pursuit of both happiness and the realization of a construct that reflects the aspirations and pretensions of owner and, sometimes, architect as well. The grand country estate was, of course, a badge of privilege and social position, as well as a living monument to a figurehead and a family. It was a house that might be designed not simply as a home, but also as an elevated memorial, such as Blenheim Palace in Oxfordshire, incomplete in 1722 when the Duke of Marlborough (for whom it was built) died without seeing Vanbrugh's extravagant plans fully realized. Ultimately, the great country house was consigned – largely, if not completely – to posterity and to history, becoming an emblem of the past, of a lost world and a lost society.

In literature, the grand country residence is, therefore, a ready loaded symbol filled with resonance and power. This is as true of Jane Austen's Pemberley, in *Pride and Prejudice*, or the Thornfield of *Jane Eyre*, as it is of Gatsby's mansion in the fiction of Fitzgerald or Darlington Hall in Kazuo Ishiguro's *Remains of the Day*. In Grimm's fairy tale *The House in the Wood*, the old man living with his animals in a lowly hut turns out to be a young prince cursed by a witch. The witch's spell had aged this handsome boy in an instant and turned his palace into a shack. When a woodcutter's daughter finally breaks the spell, the hut 'began to crack and rumble in every corner of the room, and the doors were slammed back against the wall, and then the beams groaned as if they were being riven away from their fastenings.... She found herself lying in a large chamber, with everything around belonging to regal pomp.'[1]

What it must be like, we think, to lose not only our youth but also a palace! And how wonderful it must be, we agree, to have them returned, and live a charmed life! But in many ways, the grand house – with all those connotations of elitism and social exclusion – has been a restrictive burden within the

evolution of the new country house, which arguably owes its life more to that wooden hut in the forest than to the prince's castle. Indeed, the new country house tends more toward another sequence of symbols, tied to the earthier flavours of vernacular farmsteads, barns and shacks in the woods. These are associations that are equally romantic and idealized in many ways, or even utopian.

For Henry David Thoreau, a two-year sojourn in his hand-built, 3 x 4.5-metre (10 x 15-foot) wooden cabin at Walden Pond, Massachusetts, was a kind of utopian experiment. Thoreau sought to strip away unnecessary concerns and social mores and establish a more profound connection with the natural world, as well as with his own essential self. We see something of this Thoreauvian quality in a new generation of isolated cabins by architects such as Geoffrey Warner of American practice Warner & Arsmus with his WeeHouse cabin concept or in Jarmund/Vigsnaes's new summer cabin in rural Norway. Similarly, the Shakers and the Amish sought to create a degree of rural isolation within their own largely self-sufficient communities arranged around a religious as well as philosophical social framework. D.H. Lawrence sought long and hard for a site for his own utopian community, Rananim, which he unsuccessfully

attempted to establish toward the end of his life at his ranch near Taos, New Mexico. Nearly a century later, in the 1960s, there followed the distinctive junk-built polyhedron homes of the Droppers in Colorado and the Farm Eco-Village in Tennessee woodland in the 1970s. These were generally idealistic agrarian rural cooperatives, isolated from standard society, and usually short-lived.

In their own idiosyncratic way, these utopians were drawn to the countryside for many of the same familiar reasons as we might be. They sought space and a sense of escape, a greater degree of connection with nature and the landscape, as well as a less frenetic, pressured and demanding way of life. And we are drawn to the imagery of barns and barn conversions, farmsteads and cabins partly because we see within them the symbolism of a more 'honest' way of living, as well as homes that seem essentially connected to their surroundings and environment.

THE NEW MOVEMENT
There are, of course, many different and inter-mingling strands that come together to form the new country house movement – which in itself reflects a renewed sense of optimism and confidence about rural life – but this sense of connection with the

landscape lies right at the heart of them all. Whereas the architecture of the hubristic great country house usually sought to dominate and subvert the landscape, the latter becoming a frame within which to view the house, the new country house has taken the opposite approach. It seeks a dialogue with the landscape in which the setting becomes the inspiration and organizing force around the design of the building, while landscaping is approached in a minimal, naturalistic way. The new country house, then, becomes a frame for viewing the landscape – a lens focussed on the natural world and the changing seasons. As Henry David Thoreau wrote in *Walden*:

From the cave we have advanced to roofs of palm leaves, of barn and boughs, of linen woven and stretched, of grass and straw, of boards and shingles, of stones and tiles. At last, we know not what it is to live in the open air, and our lives are domestic in more senses than we think. From the hearth to the field is a great distance. It would be well perhaps if we were to spend more of our days and nights without any obstruction between us and the celestial bodies...[2]

In many ways, from the days of Mies van der Rohe's Farnsworth House to Alberto Campo Baeza's Casa de Blas (see pages 174–9) or Marlon Blackwell's Keenan Towerhouse (see pages 74–9), the modern country house has been about seeking a sense of reconnection with the landscape and using architecture, engineering and technology to find ways of removing the obstructions between us and the celestial bodies, while still providing essential shelter and aesthetic pleasure.

The new country house seeks a place within the landscape. Here, in stark contrast to much contemporary urban architecture, context is everything and the architect understands that even an ordinary house sitting alone in an extraordinary landscape can assume a certain power and resonance by virtue of its isolation. As with Future System's House in Wales from 1994 – partially buried in a Pembrokeshire cliff face – the houses of Dietrich Untertrifaller (see pages 80–5) or Jim Jennings' Visiting Artists' House (see pages 186–91), the new country house respects the existing geography and topography of a site and seeks to work with it, pushing itself into a hillside rather than levelling it, immersing its body even within the ground itself.

Rather than clearing and felling a woodland arena, the new country house looks at how it can fit itself into a forested locale, as with Satoshi Okada's House on Mount Fuji (see pages 36–41) or Niall MacLaughlin's Jacob's Ladder (see pages 130–5).

Indeed the theme of immersion – in context and landscape – helps to define the nature of the new country house. In many instances, it leads to a blurring of boundaries between house and landscape, using topography and the site itself as a structural tool to help support and ground the building in its setting, as in the landscapers of Peter Eisenman or Obie Bowman's Brunsell Residence of 1987 at Sea Ranch, sinking into the earth with its grass roof, or Jersey or Peter Vetsch's burrowlike Nine Houses in Dietikon, Switzerland. At other times, as with Elizabeth Wright Ingraham's La Casa in Colorado (see pages 142–7), or Harry Seidler's Berman House in New South Wales (see pages 124–9), the idea of immersion is more metaphorical than physical, with these clifftop houses perched in

dramatic locations yet completely oriented around the views and the landscape, without seeking any sense of control over their surroundings.

The dialogue between house and landscape can lead in many different directions, becoming the determining factor in the evolution, orientation and form of the building, as well as influencing the choice of materials. The architectural response to the site may consider the theme of submersion and perhaps transparency, or combinations of the two, exploring inherent and vibrant contrasts between solidity and translucence, exposure and shelter, immersion and openness. The contemporary country house seeks fluidity of movement between inside and out, maximizing the importance of terraces and courtyards and integrated outdoor living rooms. Curtain walls, sheet glazing and sliding glass doors again help to dissolve the boundaries between the spheres of outdoors and in, until the two become virtually indistinguishable. The landscape passes into and through the house; the house flows out into the land.

this page Future Systems' Project 222 (1994) – dubbed the 'Teletubby House' – on the coast of Pembrokeshire, Wales. Buried in the cliff-side, it takes the theme of immersion to a sublime extreme.

top right The dacha is traditional part of Russian country life. Often modest, eighty-five percent of Russians are said to have a family dacha.

bottom right Château de Chambord, Chambord, France, designed by the Florentine Domenico da Cortona for François I in 1547, is a combination of French Medievalism and Renaissance flourishes.

The 'gardens' or grounds of the house increasingly tend to be viewed as an integral part of the overall landscape, partly to promote the sense of free passage between home and countryside. Geometric planting and composition is being left behind in favour of a far more naturalistic, sensitive and abstract approach. Meadow grasses and 'wild' flowers seep into the borders of the house; trees overshadow and interact with the architecture. Even Le Corbusier, after all, had a passion for trees and the dignity and beauty they lent to even the most brutal of cityscapes. From the extreme artifice of the baroque country garden, via the Georgian mouldings and adaptations of parkland and forestry, we have come to a rejection of the blatantly artificial and an appreciation of a non-interventionist approach, the idea of garden without boundaries and borders. As Luis Barragán poetically put it, 'a perfect garden – no matter its size – should enclose nothing less than the entire universe'.[3]

This synergy between house and landscape, this sensitivity to context and nature, has made the new country house a prime candidate for addressing issues of sustainability and environmental awareness. Indeed, the new country house has evolved within a broader framework of the growing importance of 'green architecture' and environmental sensitivity, as well as related movements toward organic tectonics and the resurgence of interest in vernacular architecture, with its emphasis on locally produced materials as well as regionally inspired aesthetics.

The relative isolation of certain new country houses – and the extreme nature of climactic conditions in some cases – has led architects to seek to address issues of energy and resource conservation and efficiency for both pragmatic and ethical reasons, as well as adopting as empathetic an approach to the local environment as possible. These are often houses, then, where glazing tends to be low emissivity and energy saving, solar power usage is common, rain and grey water is recycled, and where the structure itself tends to be low maintenance, even when it incorporates high-tech engineering. House building is a famously profligate, fast-burn consumer of energy and natural resources, while the architecture of the suburbs, in particular, is seen as increasingly short term and disposable, with the site itself the real point of value. Yet the prototypical new country house has sought to take a more responsible, longterm view within a rural homeland that serves as a constant reminder of the importance of ecological awareness and environmental sensitivity, as well as the precarious state of the symbiotic relationship between humankind and nature.

HISTORY

All of this stands in stark contrast to the great country house, from under whose shadow the new movement has sought to emerge, throwing off the imagery and smear of elitism, mostly seeing within its outmoded forebear something as dusty and archaic as Miss Havisham's neglected manor house in Charles Dickens' *Great Expectations*, the dining table still laid for its ill-fated wedding banquet and the gardens turned into a wasteland.

Certainly the grand country house belongs to another time and place. The 'classic' country houses of the seventeenth, eighteenth and nineteenth centuries were essentially communal structures, institutions with their own hierarchy and rules and regulations. No wonder, perhaps, that so many of those that now remain – and have use beyond self-contained exhibits – have become schools, hospitals, hotels and care homes, or have been divided up into apartments. Their upkeep and running was staff and resource heavy and the wealth needed to support them was the preserve of a small elite. They could be beautiful, seminal, extraordinary, but were also highly demanding and often soulless. As Alexander Pope wrote of Marlborough's Blenheim Palace:

'See, sir, here's the grand approach,
This way is for his Grace's coach
This gallery's contrived for walking,
The windows to retire and talk in;
The council-chamber for debate,
And all the rest are rooms of state.'
'Thanks, sir,' cried I, 'tis very fine,
But where d'ye sleep, or where de'ye dine?
I find by all you have been telling,
That 'tis a house, but not a dwelling.'[4]

The poet cruelly mocks the Duke and his architect, but from today's perspective it's hard not to have some sympathy with Pope's point of view. We can appreciate the accomplishment, the grandeur, the cleverness of it all. But is it really a home? Or is it more of a statement, designed to dominate the landscape and express Marlborough's wealth and accomplishments in highly visible, lasting form? 'Posterity when they view in this house the trophies of the Duke of Marlborough's fame, and the glory of his achievements will not celebrate his name only; but will look on Blenheim House as a monument of the generous temper of the English nation', wrote Daniel Defoe in 1726.[5] Blenheim and its kind are surely the dominatrix of the countryside, demanding attention, praise and passion.

Of course, the classic great country house, *palazzo*, *schloss* or château of the Western world grew out of a tradition that was essentially about defence and protection. The castles and castellos of Medieval Europe were often built on raised sites, mounds and hilltops, and crenellated, towered and moated for pragmatic reasons. In Britain, a number of these early castles were later remodelled into more 'progressive' family seats, such as Arundel Castle in Sussex, with its Medieval shell rebuilt in the late nineteenth century – a period of a resurgence of interest in Medievalism – or Bolsover Castle in Derbyshire, a Middle-Age fortress turned into a country house in the seventeenth century.

The idea of periodically reinventing a great country house was commonplace, with buildings adapted, rebuilt or scaled down according to 'fashion',

desire and necessity. Longleat in Wiltshire, for instance, began life as a Medieval priory and was reinvented four times by Sir John Thynne between the 1540s and 1580s, each incarnation grander than the last. Audley End in Essex, once the country seat of Charles II, began shrinking in the eighteenth century as sections of the house were removed.

Indeed, the burden of maintaining a large country estate, with all of its associated staff, could be crippling. During the eighteenth and nineteenth centuries a number of English country houses – such as Bradgate Hall in Leicestershire, Horseheath Hall in Cambridgeshire and Brome Hall in Suffolk – were either demolished or left to fall apart, having become superfluous or too onerous to maintain. In the first half of the twentieth century the great country house lurched into crisis as land values fell and taxation rose.

In his introduction to the 1959 edition of *Brideshead Revisited* – now transformed in most people's minds into Vanbrugh's Baroque/Neoclassical fusion, Castle Howard – Evelyn Waugh talks thus of the crisis of the 1940s, when he published his novel:

It seemed then that the ancestral seats which were our chief national artistic achievement were doomed to decay and spoilation like the monasteries in the sixteenth century. So I piled it on rather, with passionate sincerity. Brideshead today would be open to trippers, its treasures rearranged by expert hands and the fabric better maintained than it was by Lord Marchmain.[6]

Between the First and Second World Wars, more than 450 country houses were stripped and demolished, with parts and features of some turning up in unexpected places – pieces of Basildon Park reappeared in the Waldorf Astoria in New York, for example. Only the advent of the National Trust's Country Houses Scheme of 1937 began to offer a lifeline to British classic houses under threat. The English experience of building, resurrection and disaster was paralleled, more or less, in other European countries, such as France, Germany and Italy, where the ruination of war also took a heavy toll architecturally, as well as in so many other ways. In France many chateaux were rebuilt in the 17th and 18th centuries, layering new facades and structures over medieval fortress-style archietcture, as at Missery, Burgundy, rebuilt in the 1760s but with moat and defensive corner towers retained, or Montgeoffroy in Anjou, remodelled a decade later. Other donjons – or keeps – were demolished in favour of a less intimidating form of architecture suited to a new breed of 'maisons de plaisance'. The Revolution saw the destruction and confiscation of a relatively small number of chateaux within the overall context, as the nobility sought a low profile or ways of transferring property between family members. But, as in England, the 20th century saw a marked deterioration of not just the fortunes of the heirs of the nobility but the French grand country house.

Indeed, today it is still difficult to disassociate Palladianism and Neoclassicism from the great country house. In Britain, a new generation of more modestly scaled yet still substantial country houses are being built in a Neoclassical manner by 'contemporary' architects such as Quinlan Terry and Robert Adam, while even architecturally open and experimental parts of the United States, such as the Hamptons, seem to see a new pair of mock Palladian villas for every decidedly modern equivalent. An exhibition on The New English Country House at the Royal Institute of British Architecture, London, in 2003 presented twenty-six designs. Of these half are Neoclassical reinterpretations by architects such as Terry, Adam and Julian Bicknell that stand in stark contrast to a number of futuristic, forward-thinking and experimental schemes by the likes of Ushida Findlay and shedkm.

One can recognize the beauty of the architecture in both camps, yet one has its feet decidedly in the past, while the other seeks to reinvent the new country house for today and reflect a contemporary way of living and an evolutionary step onward that carries with it the lessons and inspirations of the Modern movement. If there is a Neoclassical conceptual gem from the grounds of the traditional country house that *does* seem relevant to the genesis of the truly contemporary, neo-Modern country house, then perhaps it is the humble belvedere, where appreciation of the landscape and true interaction between countryside and structure was key.

The development of the contemporary country house actually owes much more to the cabin and its cousins and to the general resurgence of interest in vernacular methods, structures and forms. If the great house was a statement of wealth, artifice and refinement, then the architecture of farmstead, barn, mill and country cabin was a much more organic, instinctive, raw and unpretentious affair of the soul. These were structures sourced in function, utility and common sense with a pragmatic approach to their position in the landscape and to their construction.

The barn, for instance, was often built of local timber or stone cleared from the fields, giving it an organic sense of connection with the countryside. It was practically positioned in the landscape so as to offer shelter from the elements, while also offering ease of access. It was devoid of decoration or excess, simple and unadulterated, but with a beauty of proportion and line. Long dismissed as irrelevant by the architectural profession, barns and other vernacular buildings were reassessed from the 1960s

onward, as architects began to see the value and drama of such buildings, as well as their positive sense of solidarity with their surroundings. Contemporary houses such as those of Dietrich Untertrifäller, Ivan Cavegn (see pages 24–9) or James Gorst's superlative Whithurst Lodge in Sussex or Reiner Kaschl and Heide Mühlfellner's Steffen House near Salzburg owe a conscious debt to barn aesthetics, which have also increasingly drawn the attention of those interested in converting and moulding existing barns into free-flowing, open-plan homes that splice modernity and tradition.

Many country estates, haciendas and plantations placed the great house and the vernacular side by side, of course, with the estate also holding workers' cottages, dowry houses and farm buildings. This was a collision of cultures, a high contrast between opposite ends of the social spectrum mirrored in brick, stone and adobe – a social and architectural microcosm. These remained two worlds apart until the evolution of a distinct middle class with the wealth and opportunity to create a new society and a new architecture in between, which fast developed in the Georgian and Victorian eras. In France, chartreuses or lodges, often a union of large country house and farmstead, offered the wealthy middle class family an alternative to the chateaux from the 18th century onwards. In Russia the dacha, which began life as a rural escape for a court elite, became accessible to the mercantile class in the 19th century. Still a symbol of privilege, they were a welcome summer retreat from the growing, growling cities of Moscow and St Petersburg an hour or two's ride from the urban sprawl. Indeed many were eventually swallowed by the tide of suburbia.

The Arts and Crafts movement contained an intrinsic proclivity to the countryside and to nature as an antidote to the growing urban sprawl of Western cities. The aesthetic shift contained within Arts and Crafts also made it an important bridge to the Modernist revolution. Frank Lloyd Wright, for instance – one of the most important influences upon the formation of the new country house – emerged from under the umbrella of the Arts and Crafts movement. Wright spent a part of his childhood growing up and

top left Philip Webb's Red House (1859), Bexleyheath, UK, was built for his friend and colleague William Morris. The collaborative house, inside and out, became an icon of the Arts and Crafts movement.

bottom left Arguably the most famous and influential country house of the twentieth century, Frank Lloyd Wright's Fallingwater (1935), Bear Run, Pennsylvania, USA, is a homage to its setting and to the natural world.

top right Le Corbusier's Villa Savoye (1931), Poissy, France. The slender pilotis lift the main living spaces into the air to maximize the views and enhance the flow of light.

top middle right UN Studio's unconventional Mobius House is a vision of concrete and glass in an idyllic, forested setting north-east of Amsterdam.

bottom middle right Philip Johnson's Glass House (1949), designed as his own home in New Canaan, Connecticut, USA. Few such modestly scaled buildings have had such a worldwide influence.

bottom right The Kaufmann Desert House (1947), Palm Springs, California, USA, by Richard Neutra. Built on the edge of the town, the house connects with the desert plains and the mountains beyond.

working on his uncle's farm in Wisconsin, appreciating the work of Thoreau and Walt Whitman. He had a romantic love for nature and the countryside, and his work, famously, sought inspiration not only from advances in engineering and materials, but also from the landscape. His Prairie Houses used a *piano nobile* concept to maximize the views as he looked to deconstruct typical domestic box-like forms and introduce open planning, while Fallingwater (1936) seemed almost to become a part of the land itself.

Fallingwater has become one of the great, iconic houses of the last century. While many might think of Modernism as a primarily urban project – conjuring up images of Le Corbusier's Unité d'Habitation in Marseilles and of the brutalist, imitation tower blocks that dehumanized cities around the world – the most powerful, defining images of the Modern Movement lie in a small number of beautiful and quite revolutionary country houses. Such retreats were all the more powerful for their isolation and were built at a time when the great, classical country house was in danger of desolation.

Le Corbusier's Villa Savoye (1929) appears to hover in a green field outside Paris, near Poissy, supported by its pilotis and incorporating terraces and decks within its outwardly rectangular form. Mies van der Rohe's Farnsworth House (1950) is an extraordinary floating glass box – an 'x-ray house', which allows the landscape to pass in and through it. Add to the list Philip Johnson's Glass House (1949), Curzo Malaparte and Adalberto Libera's Casa Malaparte (1941), Charles and Ray Eames' Case Study No. 8 (1949), Robert Mallet-Stevens' Villa de Noailles (1933), Eileen Gray's Villa E-1027 at Roquebrune (1929), Richard Neutra's Kaufmann Desert House (1947), Louis Kahn's Esherick House (1961) and so on. These are pioneering Modern country houses and embody a series of revolutions – social, technological, spatial – that changed the way we all live.

The grand houses of the Arts and Crafts movement often maintained an upstairs/downstairs culture, with service areas such as kitchens and laundries the orbit of housekeepers. Electricity, plumbing and heating systems were all in

top Alvar Aalto's Villa Mairea (1939), Noormarkku, Finland, fused vernacular elements and references with contemporary ideas and innovations to create a new Scandinavian country house.

above Luis Barragán's San Cristóbal stud farm (1968) in Los Clubes, near Mexico City, reinvented the Mexican hacienda in the form of a lyrical compound bathed in light, colour and water reflection.

their infancy and materials like steel and aluminium relatively new and unexplored. Fifty years on and the house was a completely different entity, reshaped in every sense. Reinforced concrete, steel frames and curtain walls opened up a new world of structural possibilities, while more compact houses went open plan, with kitchens integral, bathrooms essential and increasingly luxurious, and mechanization changing the way people lived and worked decade by decade.

The shift was extraordinary, and the impact of the iconic Modernist country house continues to shape architecture, becoming an essential bookmark in our frame of reference. The influence of these houses cannot really be underestimated and many still have a feeling of striking freshness and contemporary relevance, laying down a template of contextuality, transparency, connection between house and landscape, simplicity, rawness and immersion. Shigeru Ban (see Naked House, pages 180–5) talks of the Farnsworth House as 'a revolutionary work that took Western architecture, previously enclosed by masonry walls, to the realization of interior/exterior continuity by means of a glazed exterior'.[7] For Carlos Ferrater (see Casa Tagomago, pages 162–7), the Villa Savoye 'is comparable to the first printing press'.[8]

At the same time, the Modern movement was also starting to draw widely on vernacular references and organic forms and reinterpret them within a contemporary aesthetic. Aalto's Villa Mairea (1938), for instance, was a wood-clad modern country retreat, drawing on the Scandinavian timber tradition. Luis Barragán, in Mexico, reinvented the adobe walls of the pueblos in concrete and reimagined the hacienda in the form of the sublime San Cristóbal stud farm (1968), with its fountains and pink-painted monolithic walls. From being dismissed as an irrelevance, the vernacular became another source of inspiration in contemporary design, reinventing the past as the country house pushed forward.

Everything, it seemed, was possible. The Modern country house delighted in making up its own rules and then breaking them. And criticism of the country house, when it came, sounded familiar. The brutalist

tower blocks and cities in the sky of urban Modernism were derided as degrading, while the Modern country house was condemned as elitist and peripheral. Many of these iconic dreams were, after all, weekend houses and country escapes.

But today, while the influence of these seminal homes is still very much with us, the economics have started to change. It's now possible to say that a bespoke contemporary home can be built for the price of a decidedly average, off-the-peg equivalent. And imagination and innovation continue to make the new country home one of the most eloquent and exciting of propositions, with a treasure trove of diversity from organic, eco-friendly structures to vernacular-inspired houses to experimental threads of futurism. The one-off retreat continues to be an engine of architectural change, particularly in space-rich parts of the New World less troubled by planning restrictions and a large heritage stock of period country homes.

THE PRESENT

Planners and certain architects who continue to dismiss the country house as elitist and distracting, who insist our real concern should be dealing with housing shortage, providing social housing and dealing with the growing pressures of all kinds upon our cities, are guilty of condescension to the rural population. Indeed the countryside may be pastoral, but it is no longer parochial, with an increasingly design-conscious, demanding and multi-cultural community, many of whom have a fluid lifestyle, travelling, commuting and exposing themselves to a wide breadth of influences and ideas. They lead the growing demand for an alternative to conversions and to conveyor-belt, developer-led period pastiches and kit houses, which are choking many rural areas. Indeed, the new country house movement has to address the poverty of contemporary rural architecture and lack of choice.

At the same time, the whole notion of country living is experiencing a marked renaissance. Partly, this is reaction to the increasing sense of dissatisfaction with the urban experience and the mediocrity of suburbia. Many cities are struggling in terms of infrastructure and congestion, while the increasing scale of the world's supercities makes them ever more difficult to navigate and understand. As growth spreads along motorways and arterial routes and the suburbs push outward, it is becoming hard to tell where one city ends and another begins. As Kenneth Frampton puts it, 'There is no longer any clearly perceivable distinction between the city proper and the blur of the surrounding hinterland into which it continually drains its energy.'[9]

There is also a growing feeling of claustrophobia about city living, as the pressure on personal and communal space intensifies. Space is the great luxury of the urban world, so expensive yet so essential. We live in and among architectural statements and surprises, yet can't afford a modest garden. There is a growing sense of dissociation from the natural world and disaffection with the city as a place for constant living and, in particular, as a place to raise a family. No wonder that the whole notion of escapism is being taken so seriously, as city dwellers look for weekend retreats or head off to the country full time. In the UK, around 100,000 people a year are relocating from urban areas to the countryside, moving in the opposite direction to the mass migrations of the industrial age. The US census of 2000 suggested that urban America overall was continuing to grow but that super cities were beginning to shrink while the rural population had expanded by around 6%. Country dwellers, meanwhile, are more intent than ever on preserving and protecting the rural

environment and recognizing the importance of sustainability and carefully moderated development.

The country life renaissance combines the pragmatic need for space and light with the romantic love of rural living and the natural world. There is a sense in which a romantic view of the countryside lives in residual collective memory, embedded in folkloric myth. There is a touch of Thoreau in all of us as we seek essential metaphysical sustenance from the natural world. Wordsworth recognized in nature '...The anchor of my purest thoughts, the nurse,/The guide, the guardian of my heart, and soul/Of all my moral being.'[10] A hundred years later John Ruskin wrote of '...all men of true feeling delighting to escape out of modern cities into natural scenery: hence... that peculiar love of landscape, which is characteristic of the age'.[11] Today, we still warm to these sentiments.

Of course, reality seldom lives up to the romantic preconceptions of our own minds. But the wholesale revival of interest in country life gives new impetus to the ongoing evolution of the new country house. These are not machines for living in, but intelligent, bespoke, organic homes, which mould and flex to suit our lifestyles. As well as seeking connection with the landscape, they offer fluid, open-plan living space and cater for the rise and rise in home working. They challenge conventional layouts and living arrangements, adapt to new technology and allow freedom of expression. These are unique, individual homes, suited to their rural context and a contemporary way of living.

The lifeblood of the new country house is its very diversity, from the simplicity of organic and vernacular-inspired homes to the complexities and inventiveness of more experimental and groundbreaking structures. But the new country house is bound by common themes of contextuality, sensitivity and sustainability, as well as marked by rawness and integrity. It seeks to move beyond the cliché and fashion-led focus of many urban interiors to create a less pretentious, perhaps more idealistic, space. It aims for a life-affirming relationship with the natural world, a sense of connection. It looks to remove once and for all the distance between hearth and field.

[1] Jacob and Wilhelm Grimm, 'The House in the Wood', *The Complete Illustrated Stories of the Brothers Grimm*, Chancellor Press, 1984.

[2] Henry David Thoreau, *Walden*, Penguin American Library, 1983.

[3] Luis Barragán, Acceptance Speech for the Pritzker Prize, 1980, quoted in *Luis Barragán*, by René Burri, Phaidon, 2000.

[4] Alexander Pope, 'Blenheim Palace', collected in *The Faber Book of Landscape Poetry*, edited by Kenneth Baker, Faber & Faber, 2000.

[5] Daniel Defoe, 'A Tour Through England and Wales', quoted by Adrian Tinniswood in *Country Houses From the Air*, Phoenix, 1994.

[6] Evelyn Waugh, *Brideshead Revisited*, Penguin, 1962.

[7] Shigeru Ban, *Introduction to Shigeru Ban*, by Emilio Ambasz, LaurenceKing, 2001.

[8] Carlos Ferrater, Interview with Antonio Pizza, *Carlos Ferrater: Works and Projects*, Ed. Massimo Preziosi, Electa, 2002.

[9] Kenneth Frampton, *Steven Holl, Architect*, Electa, 2002.

[10] William Wordsworth, 'Lines Composed Above Tintern Abbey', collected in *The Faber Book of Landscape Poetry*, Ed. Kenneth Baker, Faber & Faber, 2000.

[11] John Ruskin, 'The Stones of Venice', collected in *Selected Writings*, Everyman, 1995.

right Perched on the hillside and accessed by an iron footbridge, Mario Botta's House at Riva San Vitale (1973), Ticino, Switzerland, has views of mountains and Lake Lugano.

far right Simon Ungers' rusting steel T-House (1994), Wilton, New York, USA, is a sculpted house sitting amid a 44-acre (18-hectare) woodland site. The upper level is a library.

ORGANIC

1

These earthbound and landscaping buildings, with a sensitivity to site and landscape, are organic houses that tend toward a natural palette of materials: stone, timber, adobe. But these familiar elements are constantly being reinterpreted in new and surprising ways within striking, contemporary structures, and juxtaposed with innovative engineering and fresh, modern aesthetic choices. Organic doesn't have to mean archaic or even traditional, but points the way toward a more cohesive, unobtrusive and respectful approach to our natural surroundings, often in tandem with an emphasis on sustainability and ecological awareness. This is the new country house less as statement, more as a subtle and sensitive form of expression.

MOLEDO HOUSE
SOUTO DE MOURA ARQUITECTOS, Moledo, Portugal 1998

The Portuguese architect Eduardo Souto de Moura is well respected for his reinterpretation of Portuguese vernacular architecture, splicing the granite walls of Iberian traditionalism with modernity and minimalism. The result is a form of contemporary organic design, well expressed in the Moledo House, which appears anchored to the stone-walled terraces of a bucolic, quiet hillside with views across the ocean.

Eduardo Souto de Moura has etched his reputation in stone. Particularly Portuguese granite, which has been re-appropriated from the past within highly contemporary buildings flavoured by abstraction, enhanced by sensitivity to landscape and setting, and emboldened by juxtapositions between the timeless textures of stonework and the striking freshness of concrete and glass.

Born in Oporto, Souto de Moura worked with Álvaro Siza, the godfather of Portuguese Modernism, in the 1970s, before establishing his own practice. The two architects share an awareness of local building techniques and craftsmanship, as well as a solid understanding of the importance of site and situation. Souto de Moura's sensitivity to context and his ability to reinterpret and rethink Portuguese stone-working artisanship have found expression in

right Through the transparent heart of the house, the eye travels to the rock face beyond, forming a sense of cohesion with the granite walls and stone-flagged terrace.

far right The organic textures of the stonework, facing the concrete walls of the house, tie in with the rough and raw quality of the original retaining walls of the site's agricultural terraces.

roof plan

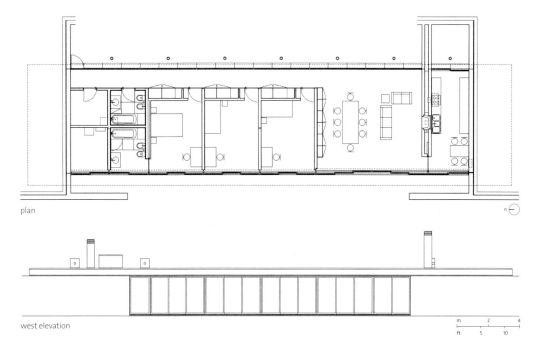

plan

n ⊖

west elevation

m   2   4
ft   5   10

urban contexts and large-scale projects, such as his tender reworking of the ruins of the convent of Santa Maria do Bouro into a new state-run hotel.

Yet Souto de Moura's country houses are perhaps the most seductive of his works. This house near the town of Moledo, in Northern Portugal, also reinterpreted and adapted existing ruins to powerful effect. The site forms part of a series of agricultural terraces climbing a hillside, stabilized by retaining walls. Also visible were the ruined remains of a seventeenth-century building. Here, the architect's client, António Reis, decided to build a holiday home for himself and his family. Souto de Moura began a seven-year programme of adaptation and modification, beginning with the reconstruction of

the overgrown hillside with new retaining walls, foundations and a platform for the new house, which together cost more than the house itself. The end result was a total reinvention of the original ruins into a new home, which seemed to become a part of the landscape itself, emerging from the terraces with subtlety and grace.

Concrete supporting walls were faced with granite in a way that matched the outward appearance of the retaining buttresses, which helped to form the old agricultural terraces, creating a natural tie between the old and the new. Yet the solidity of these walls, which anchor and envelop the ends of the building and form a partial façade, was contrasted with a strong element of transparency

left The house almost disappears within the ziggurat formation of the old agricultural terraces, while woodland at the summit of the hillside reduces any sense of exposure.

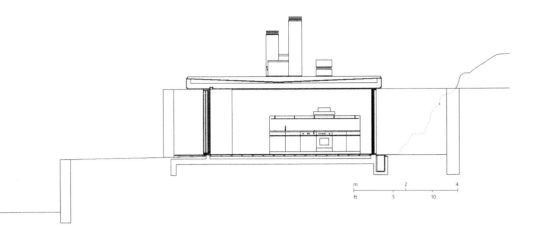

section

left A long passageway at the rear of the house offers access to bedrooms and living space, while the dramatic curtain wall invites in the rock face and sucks in sunlight.

within the elongated, single-storey form of the house, which was partly dictated by the site.

To the front of the building, overlooking the Atlantic ocean, runs a bank of glazing, with sliding glass doors opening out from the open-plan living and dining room to a modest deck and terrace. To the rear of the building there is another long stretch of glass, providing views of the exposed hillside rock, which is lit up in the evenings. There is enough separation between the glass skin and solid stone to create a light well, which helps illuminate the interiors. Within the open-plan parts of the house, then, glazing to the front and back of the building allows the eye to pass through the structure to the grey, organic surfaces beyond.

Internally, the space is divided within a linear pattern. With an enclosed kitchen at one end of the house, and service areas, including two bathrooms, at the other, the central section becomes a contrast between the openness of the living/dining room and the enclosure of three similarly sized bedrooms, accessed by a long passageway at the rear of the building. Many of the internal walls are clad in a smooth tropical hardwood, creating another strong organic dimension to the house, and the floors are also in timber. Detailing is precise but embellishment minimal, and wardrobes and storage space disappear into the warm surfaces of these timber walls.

It is only the concrete roof that appears to fly in the face of the natural cohesion between house and landscape. Clean, unplanted and ungrassed, the starkness of the roof stands in contrast to the rest of the house, especially when seen from above, further up the hillside. Souto de Moura's intention here was that the roof declare itself, new and unfamiliar, 'as if it had fallen from the sky'.[1]

This is a house of contrasts: between the open aspect to one side and the sense of enclosure and immersion to the other, between light and dark, between the warm texture of the materials and the intrinsic minimalism of the interiors, between the organic and the man-made. Finally, one is always drawn back to the nature and nurturing power of the granite surfaces, which effectively ground the building within the context of site, landscape and history and can only improve and enrich with time and experience.

[1] Eduardo Souto de Moura, briefing notes on the Moledo House

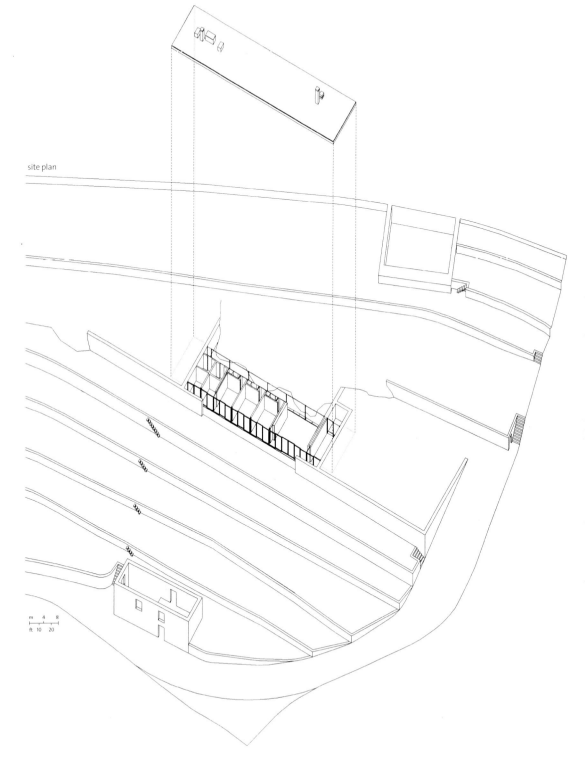

site plan

m   4   8
ft 10   20

CAVEGN HOUSE
IVAN CAVEGN, Röthis, Vorarlberg, Austria 1998

Perched on a small plateau on a vineyard-laden hillside in Austria, with views of the Swiss Alps and the Rhine Valley, architect Ivan Cavegn's own home and studio are inter-connected rectangular blocks in the landscape. One clad in larch slatting, the other in concrete slabs, Cavegn describes them as a woodpile and a boulder amid green space.

The first task for Ivan Cavegn's young architectural practice was, naturally enough, to build a house and studio for the architect himself. The commission offered a way of establishing the themes and direction that Cavegn wanted to develop, as well as seeking a sense of connection with the particularly rich architectural tradition of the Vorarlberg area, which has been particularly vibrant over the last 40 years.

Cavegn's site on the edge of the community of Röthis offered a healthy source of inspiration: a small plateau sat parallel to a modest, sweeping access road on this sloping, hillside location with panoramic views out across meadows, valley and mountains beyond. The level ground and the wealth of vineyards in the area suggested that the plateau had once been levelled as a vine terrace, an assumption reinforced by the discovery of old stone retaining walls, which help stabilize the site. All of this meant that, fortunately, Cavegn had a ready-made base into which to slot his design without dealing with any of the topographical problems and question marks common to the region.

The house and studio evolved from a sensitive response to the site, the landscape and the compelling vistas. The building was divided into two

left The concrete face of the studio, with carport above, contrasts with the larch board cladding of the main house. The two are visually connected by outward similarities in alignment and proportion.

right Parts of the main house purposefully play with the idea of transparency, allowing views through the building at key points, particularly the partially exposed roof terrace to the left.

left Glazing across the ground-floor studio and within the façade of the main house reinforces connections between outside and in. Glazing at first-floor height neatly continues into one of the roof-terrace openings.

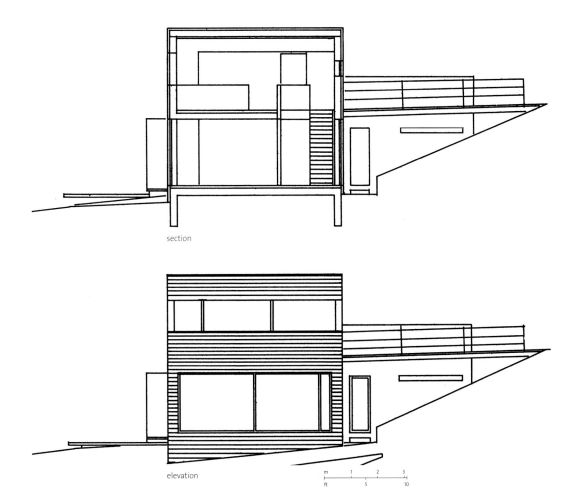

section

elevation

m   1   2   3
ft   5   10

distinct units: the main house, with a concrete framework and larch cladding, and then a smaller, secondary, studio structure, which is simply cased in concrete. These two buildings, separated by a shared access ramp and wooden walkway coming in at first-floor level from the elevated roadway and drive-in, became for Cavegn contrasting blocks of wood and stone – a woodpile and a boulder – with an organic sense of connection to the landscape. The use of timber cladding, particularly, helps tie the building into the local tradition of wooden-framed and faced buildings, reinvented in recent times by contemporary architects across the region.

The structure of the building helps reinforce the connections between it and the landscape. Studio and house present an aligned façade facing west, down the valley, with the interruption of a walkway between, plus external stairs taking you down to ground level. The studio block, which has a carport at first-floor level – flowing out to the raised roadway – and offices below, nestles further back into the site than the main house, effectively creating an L-shaped plan to the overall building. The office has floor-to-ceiling sheet glazing and glass doors pushing slightly outward to the front to meet the deck beyond, offering a panorama from desk to land. The main house adopts a fluid and unconventional floor plan, with the house accessed via a reception area leading to an open-plan kitchen and dining room with a long strip of glazing to the west. 'Here in the upper storey, I wanted to have the whole panorama, not specific, limited views', Cavegn has said.[1]

The rectangular outline of Cavegn's home is partly punctured by a series of rectangular openings

onto a large roof terrace, alongside the open-plan
kitchen/diner with vast sliding glass doors offering a
light sense of separation between the spaces. The
punctures to the terrace walls create a degree of
transparency, as well as something of a visual game,
dissolving the boundaries between indoor and
outdoor space, allowing a slice of the landscape to
pass right through the building, while also framing
essential views of the countryside.

The ground-floor plan separates private and
'public' space. Two bedrooms face westward again,
with floor-to-ceiling glazing, separated by a bathroom
between the two. The stairwell and hallway to the
rear of the building lead to a glazed access link to the
studio building, with the walkway above forming a
protective canopy. To the other end of the house is a
large living room, lowered by a couple of steps to
create a greater sense of space and ceiling height.

The minimal interiors of the main house are
warmed and unified by the use of birch flooring, with
the same timber used throughout for built-in
cupboards and units. Guests are offered slippers to
protect the wooden floor, which also reinforces the
natural, organic aesthetic within a decidedly
contemporary space. A fusion of belvedere and
vernacular farmstead structure within a modern,
forward-thinking form, Cavegn's home is bathed in
light and landscape. The interiors are minimalist, but
the effect is one of warmth and spatial and visual
wealth, with the countryside itself becoming the
focus of the architect's imagination.

[1] Quoted in *Haüser*, 6/00.

left A shutter, clad in matching larchwood, slides across the glazing around the ground floor access point, moderating the sun in summer and enhancing privacy at night.

below Cavegn's simple steel staircase becomes an abstract focal point to the transparent stairwell, leading off to the living room – two steps down to the left – and bedrooms.

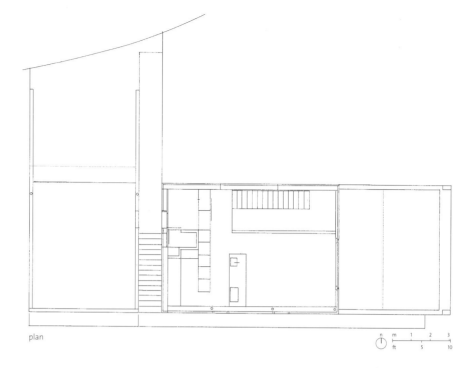

plan

SINGLE FAMILY HOUSE
BRÜCKNER & BRÜCKNER, Bärnau, Oberpfalz, Germany 2002

above The two skin surfaces of the house in larch and granite are separated by a band of glazing and framework, which also holds the entrance.

'A House in the Landscape' is the way Peter and Christian Brückner describe their design for a new family home in the German countryside near the town of Bärnau, not far from the Czech border. Using local materials and drawing on traditional elements of vernacular architecture, this is a home that sits comfortably and naturally within its surroundings.

Brothers Peter and Christian Brückner have long been interested in the reinvention of rural architecture so as to create an alternative to the characterless and intrusive housing developments that have tainted

their native Bavaria – and so many other parts of Europe – over the last 40 years. The two studied architecture in Munich and Stuttgart before returning home to the district of Oberpfalz and establishing a practice with a fresh approach to the challenges of inventing a new vernacular architecture with a solid relationship with the local environment. The Brückners have adopted a broad workload – houses, schools, churches and chapels, museums – within an increasingly vibrant regional architectural scene, which has sometimes been compared with the energy and inventiveness of Vorarlberg, Austria.

Their designs for a new house at Bärnau, on a sloping countryside site, best exemplify a sensitive but also seductive aesthetic, which forms a subtle bond with the surroundings. The house was designed for Sabine and Andreas Rösch and includes office space for a fish farm, which is spread out among a number of water meadows positioned on the sloping landscape to the front of the building, flowing down to the town. Behind the house, on the crest of a hill, runs a sweep of woodland, providing a green backdrop to the building and reducing any feeling of exposure.

To some extent, the relatively simple, unfussy, barn-like form of the house draws on traditional Oberpfalz architecture – shown in the lack of overhanging eaves to the roof, for instance – yet mixes this with a very contemporary use of technology and a neo-Modernist vein of restraint in the use of materials and detailing. Externally and internally, the key materials are local. Outside, the cladding of the house is in locally quarried, Upper Palatinate granite, while the timber boarding to the rest of the house is in larch from the owner's own woodland. Instantly, the use of these two elements connects the house organically to its surroundings, while between the two lies a borderland of glazing, which allows light to filter deep into the building and offers views across the valley. The larch boards also carry over almost seamlessly to the roof of the

right The interiors continue the theme of raw simplicity, with larch used for floors and built-in elements, such as the desks. Lime plaster walls help reflect light through the space.

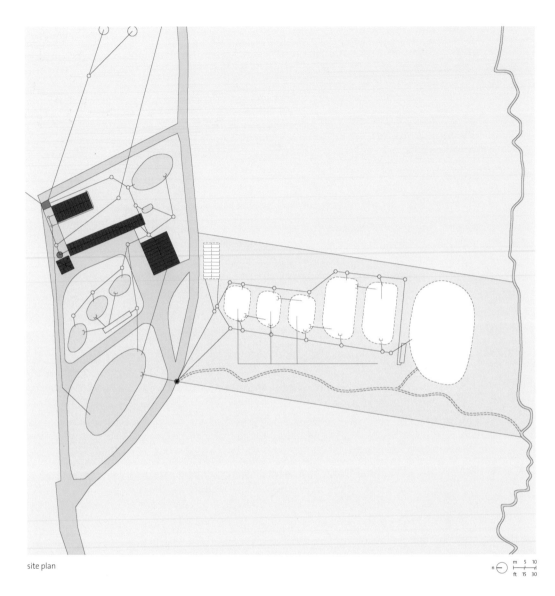

site plan

n | m 5 10
ft 15 30

building, creating a neat sense of cohesion and simplicity. 'The materials follow the example of traditional wooden structures built on granite stone foundations,' says Christian Brückner. 'The building is really our answer to the central question of which building belongs to which place? A country house should be deeply rooted in the landscape and grow out of the topography.'

The natural skin of the building conceals the solid concrete construction techniques, with the ground and first floor resting on a sunken box foundation cellar, providing service space. Yet the

interiors continue the central themes of the building, reacting to the landscape, drawing in light, and using a sympathetic palette of materials, such as granite for the bathroom and reception areas and larch for floors, selected walls and built-in furniture and units. Underfloor heating and wood-burning stoves reinforce the simplicity of the interiors, while drinking water is supplied by the farm's own freshwater spring.

The treatment of the gardens and landscaping was integral. The approach was to avoid interventions such as fencing, gates and formal driveways. A simple track leads to the house, while the meadowlands of

right Landscaping around the house is simple and sits well with the farming context of the owner's building and business. Granite and larch blend with grey skies, while the forestry to the rear offers contrast and shelter.

the hillside seep and creep up toward the threshold of the house itself. The house, in other words, tries to work with its surroundings, to complement them rather than struggling against them. In the spring and summer, the organic grey tones of the stone and woodwork offer a natural foil to the green pastures, while in the snows of winter the house begins to assume an invisibility, fading against the sky and white ground.

Brückner & Brückner's work is founded upon a policy of site-specific contextuality, seeking an architectural response that is rooted in the landscape and locale. The Bärnau house abides by this policy, yet has a presence and a resonance that stretch far beyond any regional confines. It is the new country house as an evolutionary step onward from the vernacular farmhouse, a house with a sensitive disposition, conservative in many ways, but also undeniably beautiful. As an object in the landscape it can only be pleasing.

left As well as the strip glazing, the façade is also punctured by a sequence of glass doors, which frame views of the valley, seen here from the dining room with its bespoke furniture.

top right The gable ends of the building have a barn-like quality, unfussy and powerful. The lack of overhanging eaves and external distraction further simplifies the outline.

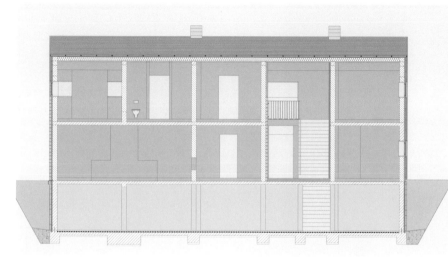

long section

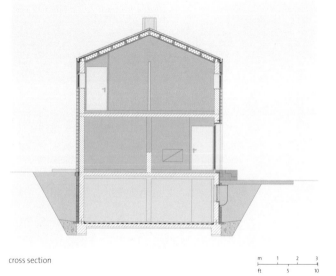

cross section

m   1   2   3
ft   5   10

HOUSE ON MOUNT FUJI
SATOSHI OKADA, Minami-tsuru County, Yamanashi Prefecture, Japan 2000

Situated on the northern foothills of Mount Fuji, within a wooded enclave that forms a summer resort community, Satoshi Okada's vacation house is an enigmatic and tantalizing building. Clad in stained Japanese cedar boards, it assumes a solid, sculptural presence in the forest, yet internally offers a wealth of surprises and spatial contrasts, as well as glimpses and hints of the surrounding woodlands.

Right from the beginning, Satoshi Okada has thought of his House on Mount Fuji as 'a shadow in the forest'. Spending a full year observing the 795-square-metre (8,557-square-foot) parcel of land in which the house would sit, monitoring the effect of the changing seasons, what impressed Okada most was the level of shadowy darkness in the woods between the ground

and the green canopy of the tree tops, even in high summer when the deciduous trees of the area are in full leaf. In this part of picturesque Mount Fuji, the tree bed is made up of birch, beech and magnolia. Here, the trees, many of them a hundred years old, are strictly protected and new building has to take preservation into account.

For the site of the 100-square-metre (1,076-square-foot) vacation house, commissioned by Sei Torii and Shunsuke Tomiayama, Okada was naturally drawn to a slim, concave, sloping spot within a gap in the trees, which tower along the ridges to either side of the building. The recessed nature of the site also meant that the house would benefit from added privacy, given that there are other vacation houses (including a rather incongruous Canadian-style log

left The house assumes a sculptural presence among the trees and nestled within the existing topography. More exposed parts of the house offer a blank face to passers by.

right 'A shadow in the forest', as Okada puts it, or a timber ship stranded in the forest – a poetic image that stands comparison with the fiction of Gabriel García Márquez or Werner Herzog's *Fitzcarraldo*.

cabin) not far away, as well as a public road on the south-eastern boundary. The plot, about one-and-a-half hours' drive from Tokyo, is on the slopes of this active volcano, and, as Okada explains:

The blackness of the building also comes from the colour of the lava, black rocks and pebbles scattered in and around the site. I wanted to represent the black mass of the building as an upheaval of the lava bed. I always think about what kind of architecture is best for each particular site and believe that each building should have an individual form suited to the surrounding environment.

On the site plan, the resulting building appears to be a relatively simple rectangular structure. Yet the timber-framed house is, in fact, a complex, often deceptive construction, rich in hidden depth. Built into the naturally sloping topography, the house is essentially a two-storey building with an austere, slab-like exterior, which also has some of the look of a grounded, angular ship. The entrance is accessed via a ramp, reaching up the side of the building, with cedar doorway and periodic window shutters set flush within the cladding of the building so that when closed they disappear into the surface of the house. Indeed, glazing and terraces have been carefully positioned to further enhance the privacy of the building and its owners. There are two key terraces or verandahs either side of the house, partially

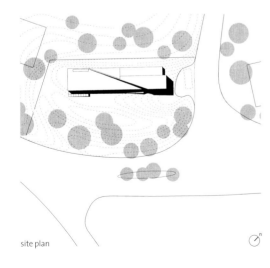

site plan

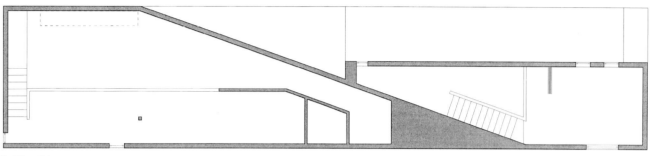

first floor plan

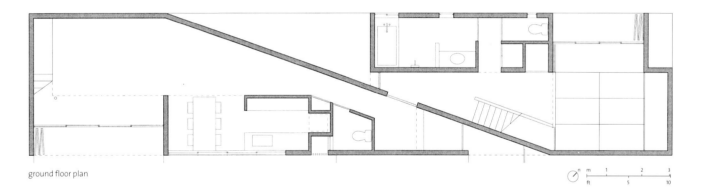

ground floor plan

subsumed within the overall structure and outline of the building, with sliding glass doors to the living room. These offer panoramas out across the woodland, while providing a degree of shelter and intimacy.

But it is clear even looking at the exterior that the rectangular floor plan of the house is dissected by a diagonal wall, splitting it into two irregular parts. The wall divides public and private elements of the house, but also plays a definitive role in the many spatial and volumetric shifts and changes taking place in the house, which find outward expression in a split in the upper level between a taller, enclosed unit holding a second bedroom and a lower segment of roofline sheltering the double-height living room

below, as well as enclosing a slim loft. Inside, the diagonal wall allows a journey of discovery through the house, from a relatively enclosed reception hall to the heart of the house: a largely open-plan sitting room, with the high ceiling punctuated by a rectangular rooflight, and dining area/kitchen to one side under a lower ceiling with loft, or gallery, above. To the other side of the house, beyond the diagonal, lie the bathrooms and a master bedroom, with its own balcony to the rear, as well as stairs up to the second bedroom.

The House on Mount Fuji becomes a masterful juxtaposition between outward simplicity and inner complexity, between organic cohesion and an internal

layering of ideas about volume and privacy. Given the limitations imposed by nearby buildings and public roadways, the house is also an exploration of a different kind of relationship with the landscape, stressing the importance of distinct and select points of connection with the woodland beyond rather than veering toward transparency. For Okada, it points to a more concentrated and imaginative approach to an appreciation of nature. Here, then, the process of assimilation involving building and landscape is subtle and controlled, but also sophisticated and enlightening.

right The diagonal line running through the rectangular house creates a series of spatial surprises and contrasts. The relatively slim entrance hall opens out into the double-height living room, with a roof light above and a slim mezzanine gallery to one side. Light is carefully edited to create shafts and wells of sunshine that illuminate the space with intensity. Floors of the guest house are in oak.

WESTLAKE HOUSE
SPACELAB UK, Oundle, Peterborough, UK 2002

With its simple cubic shape and glass frontage, Westlake House is a decidedly modern building within an isolated, rural setting. Yet its timber skin ties it to the surrounding woodland and fields, while the glazing allows a fluid relationship between inside and out. And as a low-cost new country home, it points to what can be achieved on a tight budget.

The surroundings are idyllic: there is woodland, open fields and a sense of calm and isolation, with no neighbours in sight. Given the difficulty of building a

contemporary house in England in such a spot, with all of the country's planning restrictions on rural new builds, it is a surprise to see Westlake House standing at all. Fortunately for its owners and architects, there was already a house on the site – a derelict Victorian one – which gave them a precedent for a new building. The old house was torn down so that they could begin again with something that connected with the landscape and yet was modern, open plan, flexible and multi-functional. For John and Terri Westlake it involved a leap of faith. They decided that

left With the exterior terrace deck on the same level as the internal floor, sliding back the glass doors at the front of the house allows for an almost seamless transition between indoors and out.

right The key parts of the house have been kept fluid and open plan. The master bedroom upstairs benefits from a large internal window, which looks out and through the façade to views of the nearby fields.

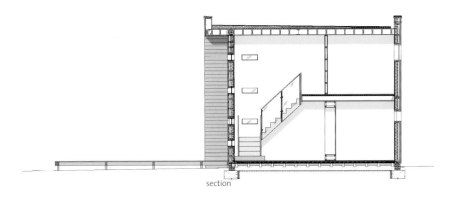
section

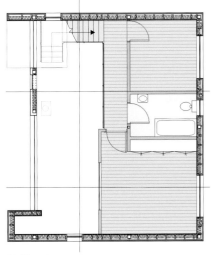
first floor plan

left A timber box sits on a brick plinth, with a skin of ply and pine over a steel frame. The letterbox windows add extra light and frame defined aspects of the landscape.

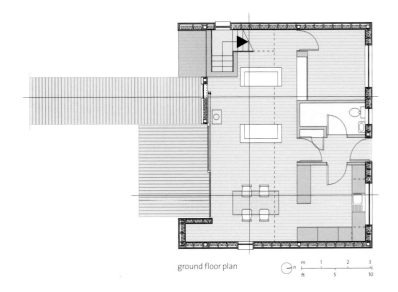
ground floor plan

for the cost of renovating the Victorian ruin, they could have something completely new and bespoke, but their budget was limited and the figures finely balanced. They relied on their architects, SpacelabUK – a young practice for whom this was the first major residential commission – to deliver a home that was not only innovative but also affordable. Andrew Budgen of Spacelab says of the project:

The challenge was to get as much space as we could in an innovative way in a one-off house. It was about using relatively normal materials in a creative way within a simple structure. It is a one-off, but in a sense it became a prototype for a kind of house that could be built on a constrained budget and partly prefabricated. That was something we became more interested in as the job progressed.

The regular box-like form – with a flat roof on a slight slope to aid rainwater drainage – and largely transparent façade recall a number of contemporary commercial and large-scale buildings, such as Norman Foster's Sainsbury Centre at the University of East Anglia, England. Westlake House takes this iconic shed-like form and translates it to a domestic scale and arena, with echoes, also, of familiar agricultural warehouses common to the area.

The tongue-and-groove timber cladding, over a plywood coat and a steel frame, reinforces the connections with the form of barns and other rural wooden structures, while also forming a material bond with the surrounding woodland and suggesting an organic flavour in stark contrast to the transparent modernity of the glazed sections of the house.

right Much of the downstairs is open plan, with the kitchen recessed to the back of the house, underneath the master bedroom. Glass and steel balustrades help promote transparency.

Hardwood cedar cladding was the first preference, but with rising costs the Westlakes were forced into a compromise and chose a Scandinavian pine softwood, which will need treating every five years or so.

The glass façade, with vast sliding glass doors opening onto a deck at exactly the same level as the internal floors, provides an easy transition between outdoors and in. Importantly, it creates a visual game in terms of proportions, suggesting that the house is larger than its modest floor plan allows, and promoting a sense of space and light. Indoors, the front section of the house is open plan, with a double-height dining and sitting area leading to the kitchen. Above this is a projecting walkway landing, as well as part of the master bedroom, which overhangs the void and has an internal window looking outward, across and through the glass façade. Upstairs, too, are a bathroom and children's bedroom. Glass balustrading for the stairway and walkway increases the easy flow of light and the visual transparency of the space.

The glazing of the façade, as well as other windows throughout, including small letterbox-style openings, constantly promotes connections with the landscape beyond and helps to frame certain views and vistas. The glass at the front of the house is coated with metal oxide, which has an insulating effect and helps to limit heat in the summer and conserve it in winter. Underfloor heating was also installed to simplify the space and maximize all available room.

The final cost of the build, including demolition of the existing building, was £135,000. It created an original contemporary family home, connected to the landscape by its organic skin and its transparency, of a kind all too rare in the English countryside. Continued interest in the project, particularly the prefabrication of many elements that were then slotted into place, proves the strong demand for such an approach in rural areas where there is little choice between period building stock, conveyor-belt estate-housing types and modern period pastiche.

ROGERS RESIDENCE
WESTWORK ARCHITECTS, Albuquerque, New Mexico, USA 1997

In the high desert scrublands of New Mexico, Westwork Architects have created a reinterpretation of traditional architectural forms, drawing on the hive-like nature of adobe Indian pueblos as well as the compound nature of rural farmsteads and Hispanic haciendas. Painted in a spectrum of desert colours, a collection of disparate shapes and towers forms the Rogers Residence.

The residential architecture of the American desert has a particular resonance and romance. The desert, by its very nature, is a particularly extreme and exposed environment, like 'the bed of a great sea that dried up unthinkable years ago...'.[1] If a country house alone in the landscape assumes a particular impact by virtue of its isolation, then a building alone in the openness of the desert enjoys a special hold upon the eye and the imagination.

Frank Lloyd Wright famously took to the desert in 1937 to build his winter home, Taliesin West, near Phoenix, Arizona. The walls of the house were made in local stone to tie in with the nearby mountains, while the design of the building was intended to echo the ancient settlement patterns of the desert. Wright's wife talked of the house seeming as though it was something existent excavated from the earth, rather than designed and built.

More recently, works by Antoine Predock, Charles Johnson, Will Bruder, Josh Schweitzer and Rick Joy have found in the desert a source of inspiration and primitive power, where buildings instantly become landmarks and surprises – unexpected forms within

left The building has an irregular compound nature, with a series of adjoining terraces and satellites. At the heart of the house is the circular form, holding the main, open-plan living spaces.

right The rounded forms and earthy tones of the house tie it into a desert landscape of wild grasses, cacti and juniper trees. Terraces, balconies and glazing serve to bring the outside in and vice versa.

left Master bedroom, TV room and study on the first floor look out and across to the mountains that border Albuquerque. Here, the first floor projects outward to meet the view.

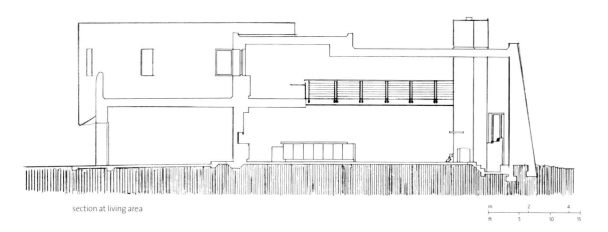

section at living area

m   2   4
ft   5   10   15

the wilderness. Predock's La Luz Townhouses or his Boulder House of 1976, all near Albuquerque in New Mexico, draw on the look of Indian pueblos and adobe structures with a smooth, rounded, organic appearance, as though emerging naturally from the earth. Schweitzer's Monument House in the Joshua Tree National Park in California consists of three different coloured blocks, suggestive of the boulder landscape, but given a high level of abstraction with irregular windows and doors, which subvert standard associations tied to domestic structures, so becoming less of a home, more desert art.

Glade Sperry and Cindy Terry of Westwork Architects have adopted a distinctive approach to a series of rural houses placed within the context of

the desert lands of New Mexico, particularly around Albuquerque. Both have a long relationship with the area, both are graduates from the University of New Mexico School of Architecture and Planning, both have a deep appreciation and understanding of the history and geography of the state. Their work also takes note of the marks, traces and architecture of earlier settlers, including Colonial Spanish elements, the instinctive and hive-like pueblos and adobe buildings of the Mexican Indians and also the stone buildings of the preceding Anasazi culture.

Westwork's Rogers Residence, in mountain foothills near Albuquerque, seeks to weave together many of these influences within a Modernist-inspired framework. As Sperry explains:

The initial inspiration for the house was the notion that the site had been occupied by previous inhabitants. The forms of the house reflect these cultures, starting with the stone structures, which are seen as remnants of the Anasazi culture. We are also interested in the notion that the various forms of the house are metaphors for landscape features in the region.

The stone masonry within the lower portions of the building, then, recalls the idea of excavating the archaeology of an earlier culture, as at Taliesin West. The layers above these stone footings are made of stucco overlaid on a wood frame, recalling later cultures, with elements at first-floor level intended to suggest the most contemporary set of interventions on the site. At the same time, the multi-faceted

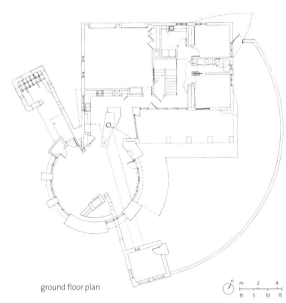

ground floor plan

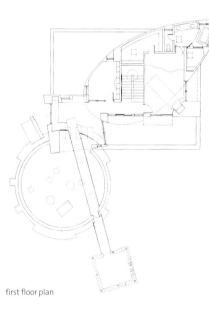

first floor plan

n m   2   4
ft   5   10   15

structure of the house, consisting of a number of intertwined and interconnected forms, also calls to mind the nature of the pueblo, while the stonework and organic adobe-like earthiness of parts of the building tie it into the surrounding landscape.

The house becomes an adventure in volume and proportion, with the main body of the house enhanced by a double-height circular central core, with a bridge connecting living space – including a study and master bedroom – to either side at first-floor level. This bridge also punctures the wall of the main building and travels outward to the rooftop terrace of a satellite stone outbuilding.

The Rogers Residence, then, has the drama of an original building alone in a landscape of special drama and power. It looks forward, seeking new forms and spatial solutions, but it also looks back, and in doing so succeeds in bonding itself to the terrain in similar ways to examples of architectural antecedents of the area, using materials, colour tones and form to successfully relate and connect the building to the surrounding landscape.

[1] D.H. Lawrence, *Mornings in Mexico*, Martin Secker, 1927.

VERNACULAR

2

Among the most powerful and beautiful of new country houses stand a hybrid group of buildings that fuse vernacular references and ideas with contemporary demands for open-plan living and flexible spaces, as well as new technology. Architects have revisited the simplicity and charm of barn architecture and farmsteads in particular, as well as the organic power of cabins, mills, alpine lodges and other rural structures. These are buildings rooted in the landscape, instinctively looking for a natural place within the topography, and seeking a sense of connection between outside and in. The vernacular offers a source of inspiration and validation to contemporary buildings tied to their locale and the landscape.

SUMMER RESIDENCE
HENNING LARSEN, Northern Zealand, Denmark 2000

above To the western side of the building stand a series of large slatted shutters, which pivot upward to varying degrees, allowing residents to control the flow of sun light and solar heat.

right The larch coat of the house will grey in time, so as to blend in further with the quiet, woodland setting. The large glazed façade of the building opens the house to the landscape.

A timber-coated summertime escape for artists, this contemporary cabin near the coast of Northern Zealand is a highly flexible, intelligent building with an organic cohesion that ties it to its woodland surroundings. The glass façade and decks accentuate the relationship between interior and exterior, while helping to throw rich light through the space.

Among the recurring themes within the work of Henning Larsen – the most widely respected of contemporary Danish architects – stands the idea of 'the house within a house', 'the internal street' and the subtle manipulation of natural light, as well as a typically Scandinavian sensitivity to context and openness. All of these themes combine within the form of a modestly sized summer escape to the north of the island of Zealand, commissioned by gallery owner Mikael Andersen.

The requested building was to be a multi-functional space – a home for visiting artists, which could also be used as a working studio and even a gallery – contained within a 100-square-metre (1,076-square-foot) structure sitting in a peaceful woodland setting, surrounded by birch trees. Larsen's Summer Residence achieved all of this in a house that is both simple and sophisticated.

57

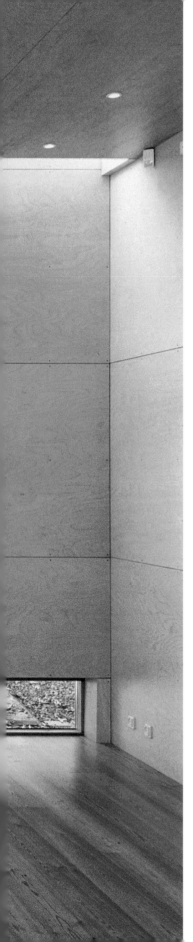

Essentially the residence is one large, flat-roofed rectangular box, with a glass façade to the front, including access to a large wooden terrace. The western side of the building also opens up when in use, with a series of top-hinged, latticed larch shutters unveiling the glazing beneath and also forming sun-shield visors when in their upright positions. Closed or open, the latticework helps cast a rich pattern of light and shadows into the building. The larch coating continues across the rest of the building – which is timber framed, with steel reinforcement – with the intention that the timber will weather in time into a silver-grey skin, which will blend in all the more to the countryside site.

Inside, the house can either be perceived as essentially one large room, or divided up into separate living and studio spaces by means of a series of sliding doors set around a central core. The brick core contains two fireplaces, opening onto living space and studio, plus a self-contained rest room and shower area to one side and a galley kitchen to the other. Closing the sliding doors, which recess into the walls of the core, can also contain the kitchen space, as well as an entrance hallway on the opposite side of the building.

This pivotal core, then, becomes almost a house within a house, enclosing the service and access areas

left The flexible interiors of the main living spaces, situated at either end of the house with a central core between them, are simply done in birch ply. Even more private parts of the house are lit via low windows and roof lights.

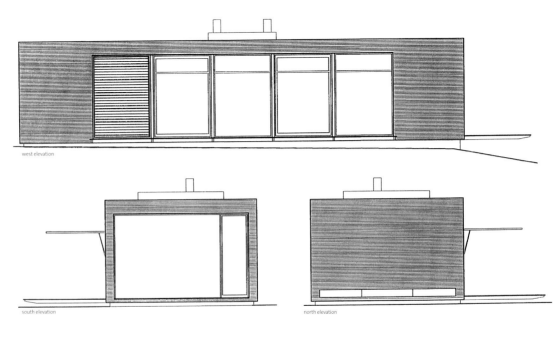

west elevation

south elevation

north elevation

plan

left Shutters on the
western side of the house
pivot upward and sliding
doors slip back to open the
house to the adjoining
timber deck. Here and at
the front of the house,
boundaries between inside
and out can be dissolved.

of the building. The doors create the possibility of
opening up internal thoroughfares, with a choice of
permutations. Light filters or washes over the birch-ply
surfaces of the interior, while blinds to the western
façade can be partially raised and shut to help control
the amount of sunlight spilling into the house.

In one sense, the building can be seen as a
highly modern, highly flexible space, well suited to
the ever-changing demands of its occupants. In
another sense, it is a reinterpretation of the summer
cabin   a modestly sized vacation hideaway that is
particularly prevalent in Denmark and neighbouring
countries. The timber coating reinforces the idea of
connection to the timber-framed building of
Scandinavian vernacular architecture. Part of the
allure of the cabin lies in its simplicity and organic
rawness, its ability to open up to the landscape as
well as to nestle unobtrusively and peacefully within
it. All that stays true of the Summer Residence,
despite the relative sophistication of the glazing
and engineering.

The neo-cabin has been a subject of interest for
many contemporary architects, particularly those –
such as Alchemy Architects in the USA (the
weeHouse) or Pentagram in the UK (Swiss Army
House) – interested in the concept of a lightweight,

prefabricated, easily transported cabin that can sit in
a wide variety of rural contexts, and even be repacked
and moved on if necessary. Larsen's Summer
Residence takes the new cabin in a different
direction, something more solid, fixed and elegant.
But all have a modesty of scale, a respect for the
environment, a sense of connection to the elements.
Larsen translates Scandinavian Modernism to a
specific location and a specific task, yet the
resonance of the Summer Residence makes the cabin
life seem an ever more enticing proposition.

Larsen's Summer Residence may stand in
contrast to the high-profile, large-scale
accomplishments of projects like his much-lauded
Ministry of Foreign Affairs building in Riyadh, Saudi
Arabia, or his recent work on a new Opera House for
Copenhagen. Yet all display, in their own ways, an
appreciation of context and setting, and an analytical
respect for functionality as well as location.

WILLIMANN-LÖTSCHER HOUSE
BEARTH & DEPLAZES ARCHITEKTEN, Sevgein, Grisons, Switzerland 1998

An illusory contemporary timber house on the edge of a Swiss village, with views down into the valley lands of the River Vorderrhein, the Williman-Lötscher House draws on the architecture of traditional block and tower houses in the region. Yet internally and externally, despite references to the local vernacular, the form and structure of Bearth & Deplazes' striking mountain retreat defies expectation.

Throughout the 1990s, Valentin Bearth and Andrea Deplazes became much respected for their reinvention of traditional timber buildings, re-examining the form and technology of wooden houses and other more functional buildings, such as schools and community centres, mostly in the Swiss canton of Grisons. Yet their work had no didactic philosophical agenda or definitive stylistic approach.

Each project was and is a response to a particular location and set of problems, inspirations and demands, linked by a reduction of superfluity to achieve an elegant simplicity as well as attention to detail and practicality. Their approach is imaginative and technical, academic – Deplazes is a professor of architecture teaching in Zurich – and pragmatic.

Before founding his own practice in 1988, Bearth spent four years working with Peter Zumthor, who has also famously explored a modern reworking of traditional materials and techniques, particularly timber. Zumthor's boat-like and beautiful St Benedict Chapel at Sumvitg – a wooden vessel for contemplation – has been described as barn-like, yet with curves and graces, and his Gugalun House at Versam literally spliced old and new, knitting a sympathetic new wooden structure to a traditional

left The topography of the site was utilized in creating a split floor arrangement, with the ground floor encompassing an entrance area uphill and kitchen and dining room lower down.

right The subtle polygon appears at its most solid when seen from downhill. The vast picture window dominating this aspect of the building is the glory of the living room.

eighteenth-century alpine house to create something new and unexpected.

With a similar spirit of innovation, Bearth & Deplazes, too, have succeeded in splicing old and new to create the unexpected. Their Summer Cabin in an isolated hillside spot near Fanas was a rebuilding of a former home destroyed by fire. The new timber house again draws on the local vernacular, but restrictions on window openings led the architects to create a flexible system of opening walls. A building that initially appears almost monolithic reveals itself when two large wall panels slide back to unveil a veranda and a large picture window looking out across the mountain panorama.

Their Williman-Lötscher House in Sevgein also subverts and unsettles your expectations. The southern face of this tall, timber house gives the appearance of a highly solid and simple structure, a contemporary equivalent of the towering houses common to the region, box-like with a steeply pitched roof. Yet walking around the site of the house – a small clearing among the trees, between mountainside and hillside on the edge of the village – it becomes clear that the form of the house is actually polygonal with only one true right angle in the footprint of the house. The house is in fact a visual game, tapering off toward its slim northernmost point, a little up the sloping site and toward the village. From this perspective the house appears a slight, modest and highly sensitive construct, which barely impedes the view out across the valley and to the mountain peaks beyond.

Structurally, this wedge-like house, built into the hillside, is a timber-framed building. The frame was

right The second-floor living room is dominated and emboldened by its vast stretch of glazing, offering a panorama of the valley below formed by the River Vorderrhein.

prefabricated and assembled on site in a matter of days. (The client assisted with the timber cladding, placing the vertical timber boards on the frame and applying a coat of dark lacquer.) Internally, the clients wanted to avoid that widespread calling-card of the contemporary house, the open-plan living space, and instead create a warren-like system of smaller spaces. The sloping hillside led to a natural split-level arrangement over four floors, so that, for instance, one enters to the slim rear of the house and then steps down to the dining room, which has a separate kitchen to one side. The main living room is on the first floor, with bedrooms and bathrooms – and also a photo laboratory and gallery – above it.

The living room is dominated by the view down into the valley of the River Vorderrhein. A vast picture window faces southward, sucking in the panorama and reinforcing the relationship between house and landscape. Other windows tend to be more modest and irregular, subverting expectation once more. A child's bedroom at the top of the house – an attic space among the eaves – is enlightened by a large window light.

Like Peter Zumthor, Bearth & Deplazes have recently been tempted to experiment with other materials, from the concrete Meuli House in Fläsch, Graubünden to their polycarbon-coated Ski Chair Lift Station in Arosa. They are now exploring the art of building in many forms and materials, always experimenting with ways and means of construction, yet their timber buildings have a continuing resonance, depth and inventive charm.

right Toward the village and the access road uphill, the house appears at its most slender and least obtrusive. The building is designed in sympathy with the view lines of others.

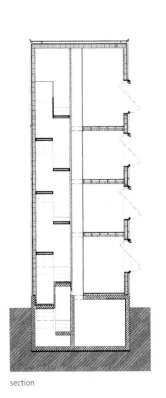

section

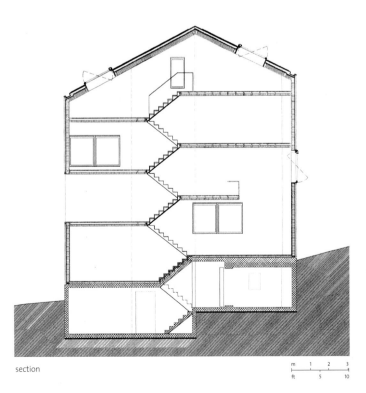

section

m   1   2   3
ft   5   10

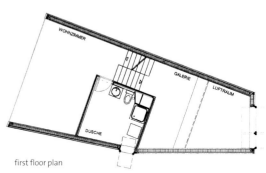

thrid floor plan

second floor plan

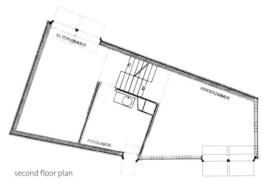

first floor plan

ground floor plan

YOMIURI GUEST HOUSE
ATELIER HITOSHI ABE, Zao, Miyagi Prefecture, Japan 1997

Constructed alongside the woodlands of a national forest, Hitoshi Abe's Yomiuri Guest House has a dynamic, angular form and a multi-functional, fluid interior. Dominated by a large, double-height living room and a partially enclosed terrace, protected by horizontal louvres, this is a home tied to the forest and to ideals of rural escapism and simple pleasures.

Hitoshi Abe is a sculptor of buildings. His work holds an emphasis upon form and geometry, abstraction and artistry, as well as being closely concerned with landscape and topography.' Architecture is like clay held between the fingers of both hands – recording their movements,' he has said. 'One hand is the human will, and the other is the condition of the

environment. Architecture is the record of the conversation between these subjects – it is the medium to reunite them.'[1]

Educated at Tohoku University and SCI-Arc in Los Angeles, Abe worked at the American office of Coop Himmelb(l)au for four years from 1988. Primarily based in Vienna, Himmelb(l)au are noted deconstructionists, whose influential projects tend toward outward complexity and abstract expression of a more extreme nature than Abe's own projects, which have a more poetic, organic quality to them. Abe was drawn back to Japan by a commission to design a new football and sports stadium for the city of Sendai for the 2002 World Cup and has based himself in Sendai ever since. Settled on the edge of

above Tha majority of the downstairs of the house is open plan and much of it double height. Galley kitchen, wash rooms and utility spaces are pushed to the periphery and tucked away.

right The lattice wall partially encloses a veranda – an ambiguous space that is both inside and out. This element of the building filters light entering the house, as though it is passing through the trees.

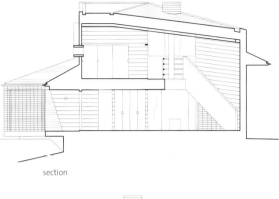

section

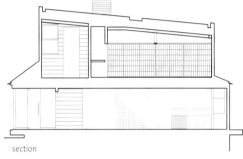

section

left From this perspective, Abe's poetic image of the house as a folding ribbon becomes more apparent, with the structure taking on a loose, abstract spiral shape that is also rather shell like.

the city, the core of the stadium is partially buried within a hillside, limiting its visual mass and melding with the landscape, with pathways and access points picking up on the contours of the hillside to the east.

The Miyagi Stadium was regarded as a successful fusion or hybrid of an international perspective and an essentially Japanese sensibility regarding form, simplicity and order. Similar observations have been applied to a number of Abe's more modestly scaled projects, including distinctive residential commissions, which draw upon vernacular references and themes but within original and contemporary structures. His designs for the Matsushima Yacht House exploited the timber boathouse aesthetic but within a crescent-shaped building that seeks a relationship with not only the sea but also the erratic topography of the site.

Abe's Yomiuri Guest House – or YG House – also combines traditional notes with a building inspired by the combination of an abstract form and a specific and delightful location. In this case, Hitoshi Abe talks of the conceptual form of a folding ribbon, placed on the landscape, encircling, forming and protecting the

above The landing becomes a mezzanine gallery overlooking the living room below. The walkway accesses two *tatami* rooms, hidden behind *shoji* screens, and a bathroom.

right A small terrace leads to the entrance point of the house. This face of the building is more enclosed and anonymous, with little suggestion of the spatial surprises to come.

interior spaces of the house, the heart of which is a bold, dramatic, double-height lounge to which all other internal spaces are subservient. Abe describes this space as a 'secondary landscape'[2], a mirror of the outside environment – partly lined in the same dark cedar boards that clad the exterior – into which more domestic concerns intrude only when necessary.

Within this multi-functional room, furniture is oriented around a triangular fireplace and a dining table, while the distorted, folded ceiling high above appears cracked by strips of glazing, which allow shafts of light into the space. A series of folding doors offers access, when appropriate, to a hidden range of subsidiary areas: galley kitchen, bathroom, storeroom, dressing room. To one side of the room a series of folding glass doors opens out onto a loggia, protected by its timber canopy and a series of wooden louvres forming a punctured wall. The effect is one of a space that is both inside and out, a halfway point where the filtered light is reminiscent of rays of sunshine passing through the trees.

A slim white staircase travels up one side of the living room, scaling the chimney breast, to a modest second level with a gallery landing leading to a wall of sliding, translucent *shoji* screens with two *tatami* rooms beyond. These references, together with the dominance of timber for walls and floors – with the white fireplace and staircase for contrast – and the overall simplicity of the internal living arrangements, link the house into a particularly Japanese

architectural tradition and way of life, while retaining an emphasis upon modernity and poetic statement.

At the same time, the house is carefully contextualized within the surrounding landscape. Like Satoshi Okada's house on Mount Fuji (see pages 36–9), the dark, charcoal stain of the cedar boarding and louvres recalls the dark heart of the nearby forest. Porch and high bedroom windows are directed to the most private and sheltered aspect of the site, while the façade around the entrance point – closest to an access road – is almost unpunctuated and far more anonymous.

The Yomiuri Guest House manages the difficult trick of creating a building of energy and dynamism – with its centrifugal, spiralling form inspired by the concept of the folding ribbon – that is also lyrical, poetic and sublime. All too often architects as interested in abstraction and pure form as Abe is tend to neglect context in all of its senses – geographical, historical, topographical – and create simply impositions. Abe allies a complete awareness of context and vernacular keynotes with a passion for experiment, theory and abstract symbols.

[1] Quoted in *10x10*, Phaidon, 2000.

[2] Hitoshi Abe, Briefing Notes on the Yomiuri Guest House.

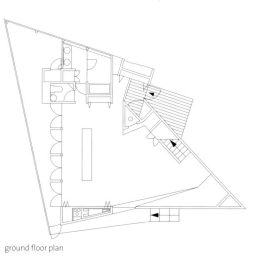

ground floor plan

upper floor plan

KEENAN TOWERHOUSE
MARLON BLACKWELL, Fayetteville, Arkansas, USA 2000

Climbing 25 metres (82 feet) into the air within a 23-hectare (57-acre) wooded enclave on the outskirts of Fayetteville, the Keenan Towerhouse rises above the tree line, with panoramic views across the green canopy to the western foothills of the Ozark Mountains and the Oklahoma plains. Standing both above and within nature, it is a seductive gateway to the changing seasons and to the diurnal patterns of the forest and the nocturnal ones of the skies.

On one level, the Keenan Towerhouse is a romantic gesture, a structure tied to imagination and memory. Its owner, James Keenan, has happy recollections of the times he spent in his grandfather's treehouse as a child. Many years later he approached architect Marlon Blackwell and asked him to create a new kind

of treehouse for himself and his family, something rather more sophisticated, which would accord with those childhood reveries and provide a playful retreat with a direct relationship with the elements and the surrounding landscape.

On another level, the Towerhouse that evolved from Keenan's brief was a cultivated, erudite response to the surrounding countryside and to local conditions and vernacular influences. This turret above the trees drew upon the drama of existing agricultural and light industrial towers in the area: grain silos, water towers and the fire watchtowers used by forest rangers. Not only the form of the tower but also the use of materials refers back to the local environment. Set within a sea of hickory and oak, the tubular-steel superstructure is partially clad in a

below Openings in the walls of the skycourt, coated and floored in locally milled white oak, purposefully frame particular panoramas of the forest and the Ozark Mountains.

vertical white-oak fin lattice around an epic stairwell. This lattice provides connections with the trees beyond, as one climbs the tower, while also allowing light and shadows to filter through. The rest of the tower, by way of contrast, is clad in horizontal strips of 'white' steel panelling, which – once again – echo the metallic sheen of grain silos and other local structures.

Internally, the base of the stairwell is a courtyard coated in creek stones and pecan shells. The stairway ascent, via a series of landings, is punctuated by a balcony window before arriving at the initial layers of the house proper. Firstly, there is a largely enclosed utility room followed by a lavatory/washroom level. Above stands the 'observatory': a multi-functional living space, for sleeping, eating and resting, with steel-framed windows to all sides, bathing the room

left From a distance the steel panelling assumes a more natural quality, with the horizontal strips on the cladding echoing timber planking. The contrasting lattice work is in oak.

above The lattice shell around the stairway allows light to filter through yet still provides a reassuring sense of enclosure during the climb to the summit of the tower.

above The summit of the
Towerhouse floats above
the treeline, rather like a
forest ranger's lookout
tower. The transparency of
the living room level sits in
neat contrast with the
outward solidity of other
aspects of the building.

in light and inviting the eye to travel outward in every
direction. The floors are in locally milled white oak,
while a three-metre (ten-foot) ceiling height on this
level is intended to emphasize the expansive horizon.

Within the observatory ceiling there is a pull-
down stairway, which leads to the 'skycourt' above, a
castello-like deck with high walls, open roof and
carefully positioned openings and hatches, which
allow appreciation of particular elements of the
landscape. There is also a fold-down table in the
skycourt, which turns this space into an alluring
dining room in the sky.

Initially, the Towerhouse proved controversial,
with locals suspicious of its unconventional nature.
Yet, while it is in marked contrast to the 'landscraping'
architecture of many 'green' contemporary rural

schemes, it exhibits a particular sensitivity to the area: only a single tree was removed for the construction of the building, for example.

Indeed, Blackwell's work is client and site specific, client and site inspired, as well as poetic and a little idiosyncratic. Born in Germany, raised in Florida and the Philippines, Blackwell comes to Fayetteville having worked in Boston and having taught architecture in a number of locations and academic institutions. In other words, his frame of reference is broad and well heeled, yet he prefers to work within a specific landscape and architectural heritage that intrigues him. 'I can get things built here', he has said. 'I had to get to know a place and allow it to shape what I do.'

Other projects – such as the hybridized, timber-framed Flynn-Schmitt Barn House, with stabling and garage space on the ground floor and living space above – have also fed vernacular ideas and associations into contemporary structures that juxtapose organic and more artificial materials like metal siding. Residential projects such as the Moore House and the 2 Square House have sought to maximize the connection of house to rural surroundings, framing views and vistas and providing platforms and viewing stations for interaction with and appreciation of the landscape.

Given its isolation and prominence, the Towerhouse cannot help but become a landmark of a kind. Yet with the sensitivity of its design it has found a way to connect with both the landscape and heritage of the area. There is a heightened awareness of context, which allows the building to operate on many different levels without seeming brash or inappropriate. As well as being appreciated by Keenan and his family, the Towerhouse now also attracts groups from the local school, who use the tower as a study centre. Like so many key buildings, it is moving from the controversial toward the iconic.

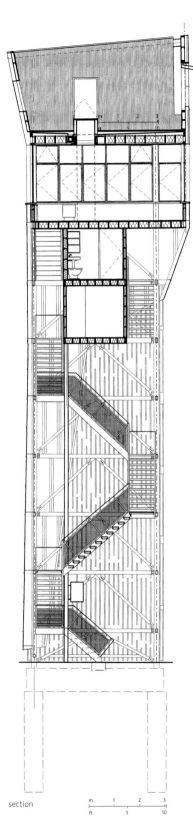

section

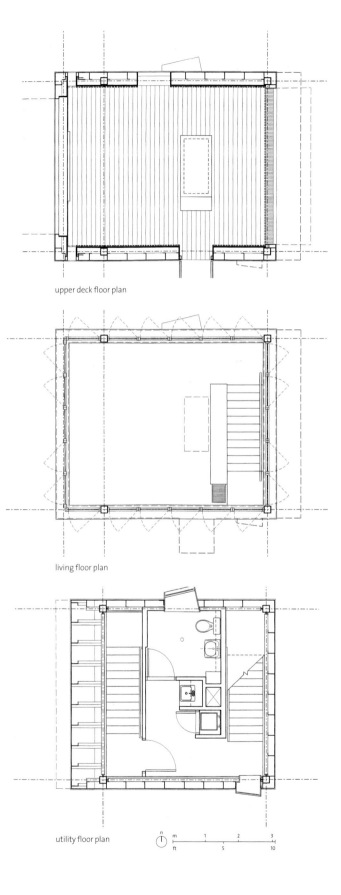

upper deck floor plan

living floor plan

utility floor plan

right The living room is a multi-functional space – an enclosed observation deck with views to all sides, as well as living room and a nest for sleeping and relaxing.

SUTTERLÜTY HOUSE
DIETRICH UNTERTRIFÄLLER ARCHITEKTEN, Egg, Vorarlberg, Austria 1998

The houses of Dietrich Untertrifäller have a strong connection with Vorarlberg, and particularly with the Bregenzer Wald mountains, with their long tradition of timber-clad building and renewed focus on contemporary reinterpretations of the vernacular. The Sutterlüty House displays all the hallmarks of a site-sensitive design responding to a spectacular location.

Once upon a time, barns and farmsteads were dismissed by architects as parochial and irrelevant. Since the dawn of the Modern movement, however, there has been a steady reassessment of the instinctive prowess of such vernacular buildings and a growing realization that they have much to teach us about relating a building to the landscape and formulating simple, pure architectural solutions

devoid of excess. Many contemporary architects have revisited the form and nature of barns and farmsteads, reinterpreting them in new homes that share an emphasis on sensitivity and sustainability. This is particularly true of the Bregenzer Wald region of Vorarlberg, at the westernmost tip of Austria. Here there is a strong heritage of timber farm buildings, barns and alpine huts, which was revisited from the 1960s onward by a loosely affiliated group of architects interested in the challenge of creating contemporary houses with a regional identity. By the 1980s, the area had a remarkable reputation for one-off, innovative houses subtly related to the unique context of the mountainous Bregenzer Wald.

Since the early 1990s, Helmut Dietrich and Much Untertrifäller have been at the forefront of the

left The house is set back into the side of the hill, with the façade facing southward, down the valley. The building is wrapped in a fir coat, which will grey and weather over time.

right The long verandas on the raised ground and first floors are reminiscent of ships' promenading decks. These decks open the house up to the meadows and valley floor.

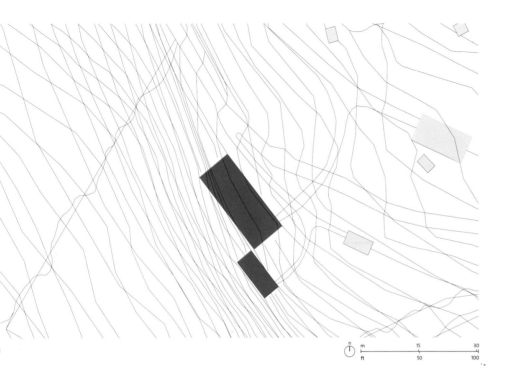

site plan

right The overall outline of
the house is simple, yet
within it are many layers of
complexity, particularly at
the point where inside and
outside space dissolve into
one another.

continuing focus upon tectonic innovation. Their
buildings share a common language and approach,
yet are completely bespoke and individually
grounded in specific locations and circumstances.
Like much of the new architecture of Bregenz and
Vorarlberg, their work is marked by the use of simple
forms and a pragmatic approach.

Dietrich Untertrifäller's work has included urban
projects, notably the Bregenz Festival Opera Hall, but
it is their new country houses that have captured the
attention and imagination of clients and critics. Over
recent years they have created a series of houses
that display a common allegiance to barn forms and
traditional Bregenzer Wald farmhouses. Essentially
these are simple, box-like structures with pitch roofs
and timber skins, but they are differentiated not only
by their relationship to site but also by the way in
which each structure is cut and sliced: each simple
barn-like form is marked by incisions to the sides, as
though pieces were missing from a three-
dimensional building block puzzle.

The Sutterlüty House is in Bregenzer Wald,
between the villages of Schetteregg and Egg,
situated on a hillside with postcard views down into

the valley and across to the mountain peaks. The
rectangular house is built into the hillside site,
adapting to the existing terrain, where the meadows
have been left open and are otherwise largely
untouched. The house runs parallel with the contours
of the hillside, its most open and exposed length
facing out to the vistas of the south-west. Here three
full storeys are visible, although at the rear of the
house, which pushes into the hillside, just two floors
are exposed. Set within the overall structure and
bodily proportions of the house are three long
porches running much of this south-west facing
length, one for each level, reminiscent of
promenading decks. These covered porches provide
terraces and balconies, which dissolve the boundaries
between indoors and out, framing the views and
pulling them back into the main living spaces via long
sequences of glazing and glass doors.

One enters the house to the rear, at ground floor
level, which also holds the kitchen, dining room and a
bedroom. The main living room is in the basement,
leading out to the terrace, with utility areas to one
side. The main bedrooms are at the top of the house,
benefiting from the best of the dramatic panoramas

offered by the building. Many of the different zones in the house are formed by sliding walls, creating highly flexible and adaptable spaces, particularly on the ground floor. Throughout, more utilitarian areas are pushed toward the more closed, northern side of the house. Both interior and exterior make use of locally sourced silver fir. Outside, the untreated fir – which will age and grey – forms a latticed skin, which also screens smaller windows and openings, creating a sense of simplicity and cohesion, as well as reinforcing the vernacular flavour of the building.

Replacing a derelict alpine hut, the Sutterlüty House is in some sense an original balancing act between the twin forces of traditionalism and

Modernism. Yet it also has a self-assurance and a natural sense of absolutely belonging to its rigorously examined context. The original huts and barns may be disappearing from the Bregenzer Wald, but there is a new generation of buildings with just as much sensitivity and sense of connection to the landscape and the mountain spill.

left The kitchen lies at the heart of the building on the ground floor, with the dining room to one side and the veranda to the front. The stairway runs through the middle of the house.

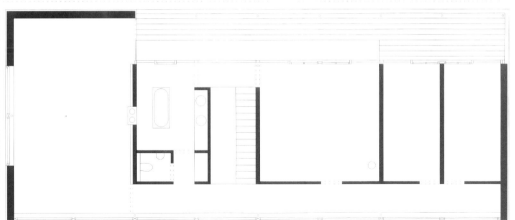

first floor plan

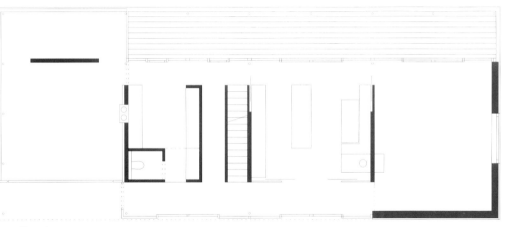

ground floor plan

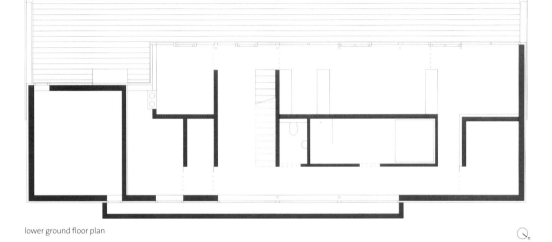

lower ground floor plan

section

m		2.5		5
ft	5	10		15

Y HOUSE
STEVEN HOLL, Catskill Mountains, New York State, USA 1999

A sculptural presence on a hillside in the Catskill Mountains, Steven Holl's Y House holds an original form but also – with its cedar cladding and barn-red coat – announces its relationship with agricultural buildings and farmsteads of the area. With its twin façades of glass and porches it also reaches out into the landscape and delights in the shifting patterns and shadows of the sun's arc.

The Y House is a reminder of the powerful imagery created by the presence of a singular house adrift and alone in a dramatic landscape, as well as the apparent fragility of such a home. Much of Steven Holl's work has taken the form of large-scale institutional projects – museums, galleries, educational facilities – yet his rural residences are among the most striking and painterly images in his portfolio. They also effectively reassert Holl's concentration upon what Kenneth Frampton describes as 'dynamic spatial conception, technological ingenuity, and sculptural form'.[1]

A number of Holl's early houses responded to and reassessed vernacular references, although more recent homes – such as the Turbulence House in New Mexico, likened to the shimmering tip of an iceberg emerging from the desert – are far more abstract, iconoclastic and experimental in their conceptual nature. There are houses, too, with a lyrical narrative, such as the Berkowitz-Odgis House on Martha's Vineyard (1988), where the outwardly skeletal appearance of the beach house was inspired by a myth reported in Melville's *Moby Dick*, in which local Indians would use the skeletons of beached whales as frames for primitive houses, coating them in branches and animal skins.

The Y House, which in some senses marks a revisitation of the vernacular themes seen in some of Holl's earlier work, also has a lyrical genesis. One day in November 1997, as Holl visited the site of the house – within a 4.5-hectare (11-acre) plot in the Catskills – for the first time, his thoughts were taken

right The house has two outward faces, with shared characteristics and aesthetics but with different characters and floor plans: bedrooms are upstairs on the right face, downstairs on the left.

elevation

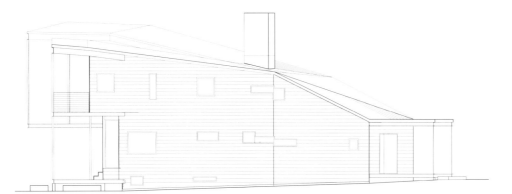

elevation

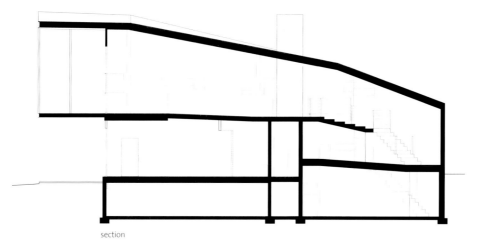

section

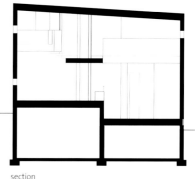

section

along by the landscape and topography and also by a forked stick, like a divining rod, which he found lying on the ground. He laid out the basic form of the house, including the porches and contrasting layers of the house, then and there in his sketch book. In his own words:

The relation of all the site elements, the long, distant views to the southwest, the arc of the sun and the circle of approach from the bottom of the hill to the top, brought forth the thought of the house circling from the arrival point as a low one storey structure and then branching up and out into the Y shape. The house literally grows up and out of the landscape, branching into the south sun, so the porches help shade summer sun out and allow

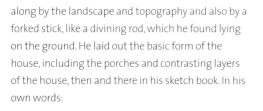

along by the landscape and topography and also by a forked stick, like a divining rod, which he found lying on the ground. He laid out the basic form of the house, including the porches and contrasting layers, then and there in his sketch book. In his own words:

The relation of all the site elements, the long, distant views to the southwest, the arc of the sun and the circle of approach from the bottom of the hill to the top, brought forth the thought of the house circling from the arrival point as a low one storey structure and then branching up and out into the Y shape. The house literally grows up and out of the landscape, branching into the south sun, so the

porches help shade summer sun out and allow winter sun in. On one side of the house night time functions (bedrooms) are below and on the other side of the Y they are above, so you have this flipped action which allows privacy and windows inside the Y space.

The house, then, appears to almost emerge out of the hillside, like a tectonic fissure levering upward from the earth, as one ascends toward it. It is effectively two houses in one, with the two branches of the Y rather like Siamese twins, sharing the same entrance way, but each having its own living space on one floor and bedroom space on the other. The northern twin is slightly larger and dominant, with two large bedrooms on the ground floor and an open-plan living space above, with its own projecting balcony partially sheltering a terrace and pool below. The southern twin inverts this arrangement, swapping the living spaces around, which – as Holl says – enhances privacy, but also provides the opportunity for differing relationships and connections with the landscape. The wings each have their own character but share a natural sense of connection and solidarity, with the ash floors throughout tying the spaces together and enhancing the cabin-like aesthetic of the building.

Indeed the Catskills is a home ground for cabins – traditional and contemporary – and vacation retreats. It is also home to farmsteads and barns – many of them painted a similar barn-red to the Y House – which are naturally grounded in the

right The two wings of the house share common access and foyers, but have their own identities and separate spaces for living and sleeping, effectively creating two houses in one. The building is given unity by common choices of materials and finishes, such as the black ash used for the floors.

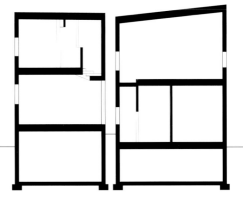

section

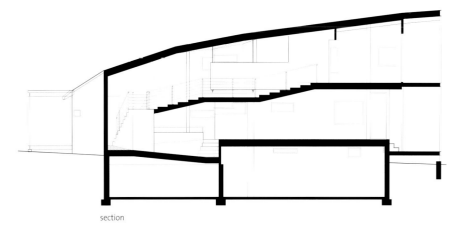

section

right The split of the Y shows the alternating, irregular window patterning to each of its branches. This, and the contrasting sleeping arrangements, provides a degree of privacy for each segment of the building.

far right The barn is coated in a red-stained cedar, while steel roof and framing are painted a matching red oxide. The colour and timber tie the building in with the ox-blood barns of the region.

elevation

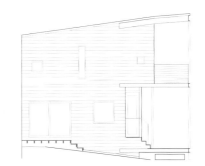

side elevation

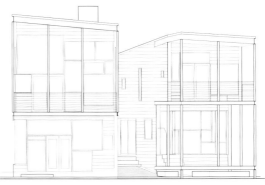

front elevation

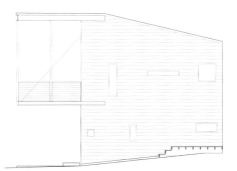

side elevation

landscape, taking advantage of topography in intuitive fashion to provide protection from the elements and practical connections with the surroundings. The Y House shares this sense of grounding, a responsiveness to the landscape and an awareness of its position in the natural order, with little or no intervention in the grounds beyond the perimeters of the house.

The client also wanted the building to be a home for his art collection, as well as – like so much of Holl's work – a piece of art in itself, a pure form on the largest possible canvas. The Y House achieves this very well, but also subverts one's expectations, playing upon the imagery of a barn and twisting it in new and unexpected directions.

[1] Kenneth Frampton, *Steven Holl Architect*, Electa, 2002.

RED HOUSE
JARMUND/VIGSNÆS ARCHITECTS, Oslo, Norway 2002

On the western outskirts of Oslo, in Norway's Lysaker River Valley, Jarmund/Vigsnæs have created an arresting home, coated in red-stained fir and placed like a beacon among the trees. Drawing upon and reflecting the design of post-war houses in the area, yet also adopting its own contemporary identity and form, Red House is a dramatic response to landscape and local conditions.

The young Norwegian practice of Jarmund/Vigsnæs, founded in 1995, has rapidly proved itself adroit in its appreciation of the powerful and sometimes raw landscape of the countryside. They have worked in spectacular locations where the climate can be extreme and challenging, taking best advantage of the sites themselves but also proving themselves sensitive not only to the elements but also to local

architectural mores and existing interpretations of Scandinavian traditionalism.

Their headquarters for the Governor of Svalbard, Norway's northernmost province, is partly submerged within a bold, mountainous landscape. It has some of the semblance of a fortress, but a protective zinc cladding on walls and roofline refers to the mining traditions of the island of Spitsbergen. Their Coastal Traffic Centre, perched on a cliff top at Kvitsøy, also has a venturesome fortress-like aesthetic combined with modern lines and surfaces. The sloping walls of the building were clad in slate, lending an organic tone to the building, which ties it to the clifftop setting but also suggests a connection to the pitched slate roofs of the houses in the village below, on the shoreline.

Jarmund/Vigsnæs' residential projects actively explore the relationship between architecture and

left The view from the veranda on the upper level of the house out into the surrounding woodland slopes is framed by the openings in the broad outline of the house.

right From downhill, the roof of the raised terrace assumes an abstract, sculpted outline. The children's bedrooms are situated on the lower floor of the building, with views out into the woods.

landscape, as well as drawing on regional references and inspirations. As Håkon Vigsnæs observes:

Scandinavia has a strong tradition of country houses. An open-air leisure-time tradition combined with easy access to uncultivated countryside has made this possible. The bulk of traditional country houses are really huts, built by the owners and evolving slowly over time. If country houses are to remain very different from general housing in the future, then they still have to reflect the owner's wish to lead a different life in the countryside, focussed upon close contact with nature, and scale should not be the main issue.

A number of the practice's buildings have updated the tradition of a rural escape, from cabins to country houses. They include Red House, on the western edge of Oslo, a timber-framed home clad in a vibrant, distinctive red-stained fir coat – the choice of the client – which stands out all the more in the snows of winter. The owner of Red House grew up in this wooded valley location, which is home to a number of post-war family houses with familiar pitched roofs and wooden cladding that are also stained in spirited shades.

In fact the client's site was once part of the grounds of his parent's home, so the area was rich with connotations and childhood memories. The design of the new house took all this into account, as well as the fact that this was to be a family home, for a couple and their three children, and that it needed to take advantage of the drama of the site, as well as responding to the demanding topography of the steeply sloping hillside.

Red House, then, was built into the hill at right angles to the slope, sitting among the pine trees with its bold rectangular form projecting outward and pointing down the valley. This sense of immersion

left Against a bed of snow, the red-painted fir skin of the house assumes greater prominence. The bright colour choice becomes almost ironic given the overall sensitivity of the house to its setting.

helps to settle the building into the site but also protects the views held by existing houses nearby. One enters Red House uphill, to the east, where the house might appear – on first impressions – to be single storey, with its long, slim, simple form and flat roof. The internal organization of space steps away from the conventional European model by placing the main living spaces plus the master bedroom on the top floor, with entry to one end and a covered terrace or veranda to the other, facing westward and maximizing the valley view. From these dominant spaces, ranks of glazing face southward with a long view through the trees and sloping terrain. The children's triptych of bedrooms plus a playroom are on the lower floor, with glazing primarily oriented to the north. There is also an additional storage room in a small basement level at the westernmost point of the building, where the volume and mass of the house is most apparent.

House and landscape appear to work together, as in much of Jarmund/Vigsnæs' work, complementing and encouraging one another. With the choice of materials, the placing of the house in its site, and the ordering of living space to promote and enhance the relationship between the occupants of the house and the natural world around them, Red House suggests how a combination of sensitivity and innovation, spatial awareness and originality can create a house that is unconventional and distinctive but that also draws upon and reinterprets established architectural traditions.

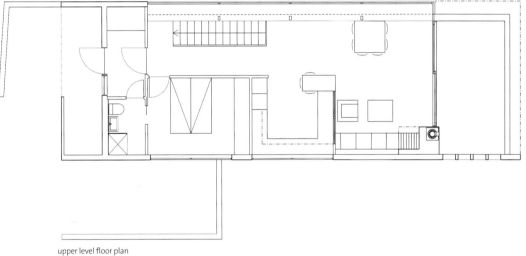

upper level floor plan

lower level floor plan

below The main living spaces of the house are largely open plan and sited on the upper level, connecting to the veranda. A fireplace becomes a focal point for the space.

right The entrance to the house belies its drama. From the access level to the rear, the building appears a box-like bungalow. The house opens out as you travel through it.

Well versed in the language of the iconic Modernist country house, these are the architectural heirs of Mies van der Rohe, Le Corbusier, Eames and Barragán. However, the new modern house does not simply draw upon the revolutions of the past, but looks to carry on the evolutionary process that was given such impetus by the Modernist upheaval. The modern country house is especially open to innovation, to new materials and technology, to challenges in engineering and structure. Even when the tendency is toward statement and aesthetic heroics, these are homes that still preserve a healthy respect for their rural surroundings and acknowledge the drama and power that their isolated position within the landscape must give them.

BÜCHEL HOUSE
BAUMSCHLAGER & EBERLE, Vaduz, Liechtenstein 1996

Situated beneath a quarry face, near Vaduz Castle, not far from Liechtenstein's capital, Baumschlager and Eberle's Büchel House is a statement building with a sensitive soul. The concrete slabs of the house resonate with the stone of the quarry, while the house was built upward to three storeys to maximize the potential of the site and avoid disturbing nearby orchards.

The work of Carlo Baumschlager and Dietmar Eberle – who both grew up in the Austrian enclave of Vorarlberg, studied in Vienna and then returned home to begin work – has a striking breadth and depth. It might be tied together by pragmatism and sensitivity to site, topography and landscape, but it has expressed itself in disparate uses of materials and very different formal exercises. They have explored brick within buildings such as their Waldeburgstrasse housing complex in Nüziders, a sweeping three-storey building spread out along sloping terrain. They are perhaps best known for their timber and timber-clad buildings, from their sculpted Hergatz timber showroom and warehouse, with an eye-catching, low-slung abstract ark-like form, to the Kern House and Wolfurt bank building – essentially glass boxes coated in larch slats to create a hybrid aesthetic drawing on both organic vernacular and transparent modernity. Then there are some powerful concrete structures, such as the Flatz House and the Rohner Port Building, Fussach, which has the extraordinary appearance of a vast

cantilevered slab of concrete, seemingly balanced in precarious fashion on a slim supporting leg.

There is, of course, further common ground between these projects, which have been born of the vibrant architectural movement of Vorarlberg and busily explored since the practice's conception in 1985. These buildings of Baumschlager & Eberle are united by a common concentration upon mass, upon formal and structural contrasts between solidity and transparency, and between artifice and nature, as well as upon craftsmanship and precision. These buildings make their mark boldly upon the distinctive landscape and conditions of the region, yet also seek connection and integration, and they are pure and unembellished, tactile and layered with texture.

far left The house sits within an orchard, underneath a tall quarry face. The three-storey structure meant that the building could have a smaller floor plan and so avoided disturbing the site further.

left The façade features banks of glazing to all three levels, each projecting a little beyond the one below. The French windows fold back to create a balcony effect on the upper levels.

right The house lies against the extraordinary backdrop of the fruit trees and quarry face. The concrete sides of the building ally it with the natural stone slab beyond.

far right The garage, tucked away on the ground floor to the east, is reached via a driveway, which curves around the rear of the building. A tall vertical window introduces light to the back of the house.

plan

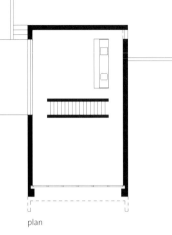

plan

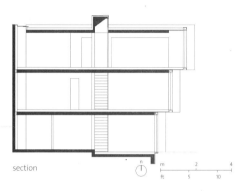

section

section

The same is true of the Büchel family house, a compact building across the border in neighbouring Liechtenstein, which maximizes the potential of its location with a tower-like, inverted ziggurat design. The first and second floors cantilever outward over the floors below, creating additional volume while offering an outwardly transparent face with ranks of French windows looking out to create vast balcony-like effects on the top floors and a seamless transition to a small terrace on the ground. The house appears to thrust outward toward the slope of the valley below and is cradled by trees and the cliffs to the rear.

The quarry cliffs offer a natural backdrop against which the house is projected like a photograph or a scene from a film. This is a house, after all, that does not try to hide its man-made, mathematical qualities, yet attempts to order and limit its intrusiveness, inviting nature to accept and tolerate its presence. 'Because the surroundings are so powerful we wanted to create a very direct and strong house,' Dietmar Eberle has said, 'and we thought the concrete would be an answer to the rock.'[1]

The house also makes the most of the gentle sloping topography of the site and is built into the bank of the slope, minimizing the intrusion of the building on the natural order. To the west side of the house a projecting terrace springs out at first-storey level, extending the dining room with additional outdoor space accessed by large sliding glass doors. The terraces serve to soften the lines between inside and out, rather like the balcony effect of those banks

of sliding doors, and so the outside seems to flood inward. Internally, the house is simply divided into two halves by a central staircase running up the middle of the building. Service areas are pushed to the more enclosed rear of the building, while the main living spaces are toward the front on the first floor with bedrooms above on the second. Light is invited through the house not only via the vast sheets of glazing to the front of the house but also via skylights over the stairwell and geometric window punctures in the sides of the building. Yet the flat north wall, facing the cliffs, is completely closed – a monolith echoing the grey stone of the quarry face.

The arresting, mesmeric quality of the sculpted mass and enigmatic surfaces of Baumschlager & Eberle's buildings are gradually drawing them beyond the homeland of Vorarlberg and into a wider context. As the Büchel House suggests, their work manages to address so many of the key issues and challenges facing contemporary architecture within buildings that are artful and distinct. There is a focus on cost-effectiveness, sustainability, contextual awareness, sensitivity to landscape and environment and an emphasis on craft and concision. Famously, the practice likes to allow its work to speak for itself. Its work is certainly making itself heard.

[1] Quoted by Joseph Giovannini, commentary on the Büchel House, architects' briefing notes.

right In the main living room, on the first floor, the bank of floor-to-ceiling French windows folds back to open the space to the landscape. The central stairwell acts as a divider between spaces to the front and rear of the house.

COLORADO HOUSE
ARCHITECTURE RESEARCH OFFICE, Telluride, Colorado, USA 1999

Characteristically, Architecture Research Office's approach to their Colorado House project involved intense study of site, context and requirements. The result is a building connected to the landscape and one that frames the various panoramas to all sides, creating a strong and constant relationship between interior and exterior and deftly balancing public and private space.

The considered orientation of the Colorado House is an intrinsic part of its success. The glazed façade of this concrete-framed building on a high mesa or plateau in the San Juan Mountains is divided into four distinct but irregular units on two levels, facing north-east toward the Sneffels mountain range 30 kilometres (19 miles) or so in the distance, as well as capturing elements of the adjacent aspen forest and the surrounding meadows. Key living spaces toward the front of the house savour this vista, while other parts of the house – a low-lying structure, stretching back substantially but subtly through the gently undulating, wilderness site – enjoy other carefully framed views of the remote locale, including the Ophir Needles to the south. As Stephen Cassell – principal of Architecture Research Office (ARO), together with Adam Yarinsky – says of the house:

We worked hard to weave the house into the landscape. Each room was designed to have a different

right Seen from the side, the house sits low in the landscape with the ascending tree line behind. The building sits within a 24-hectare (60-acre) site of meadows and woods, all at an altitude of 3,000 metres (10,000 feet).

far right Key living spaces, including the master bedroom, push outward toward the front of the house, their glass façades connecting to the landscape.

left The house relates directly to the topography of the site, with shifting floor levels throughout. The left-most wing of the house is on a lower level entirely, its roof forming a terrace adjoining the main living spaces.

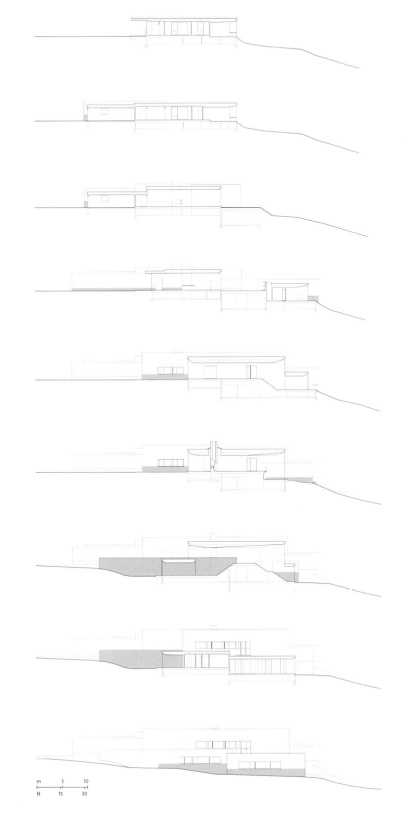

m   5   10
ft   15   30

view and we made each area of the house act as a frame for viewing the landscape. We try to make each project different, shaped by its use and surroundings. In this case, it was how the clients wanted to use the house and the views which shaped the design.

The clients are a family with a love of the outdoors and outdoor pursuits, such as hiking and skiing. They wanted a vacation home with a good deal of shared, open space for entertaining and gathering, but mixed in with more intimate retreats. And, of course, they wanted to be able to appreciate their surroundings even from within the heart of the house, which is situated within a 49-hectare (120-acre) parcel of land accessed by a 13-kilometre- (eight-mile-) long dirt track.

Having made an initial, inspirational visit to the site, Cassell began to examine how these various requirements could be related to the design of the house and how best to capture and enhance the essential vistas. He created a series of computerized topographic maps and models and used them to experiment with orientation and so formulate a way forward for the design and floor plan of the house, all tied into the various panoramas identified.

The structure is basically a single storey, but with various shifts in floor level to account for the direct topography, plus a lower wing positioned a little further down the gently sloping site. The design of the house creates a balance between not only public space and private, but also internal space and adjoining terraces and courtyards, which have a strong sense of connection with adjacent living areas. There are essentially four parallel blocks of living space, with bedrooms mostly positioned to the wings and communal zones to the centre.

The main entrance is to the rear of the building, where the entry hall leads into the congregational heartland. The large kitchen and breakfast room is a pivotal space, leading to a dining courtyard, largely contained within the overall body and outline of the house with just a slim cutaway wall as a direct connector to the landscape. To one side is the main living room and dining room – a large, open-plan space, connecting to an outdoor terrace positioned on the roof of the lower level. Unlike the other bedrooms,

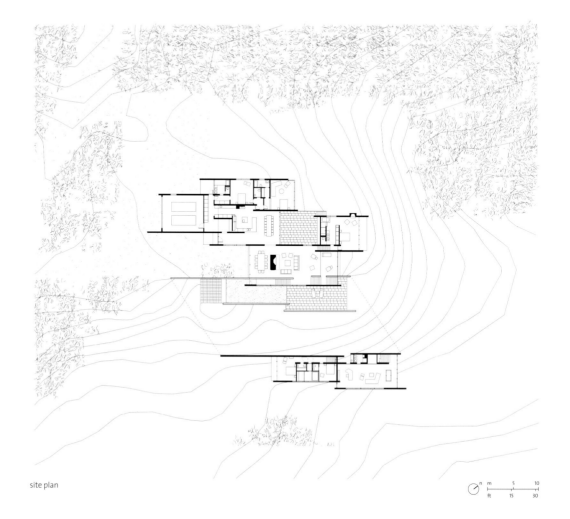

site plan

the master bedroom is positioned out on its own within the central aspect of the building, projecting out at the front of the structure and backing onto the dining court.

Finishes have a raw simplicity, with polished concrete floors and white plaster walls, to display the client's art collection to best effect. Outside, the walls that separate and enclose the irregular blocks of inter-connected living space are coated in Cor-ten shingles resting on the concrete framework. The rust colour of the shingles was selected not only for its organic appearance, but also to echo the many disused mining structures that are dotted around the region. In certain parts of the house these shingle walls slip into the house, further dissolving the boundaries between inside and out.

Much of ARO's work has tended to be city-centric, focused on Manhattan – where the practice is based – and the surrounding area, with a broad range of projects, commercial and residential, plus exhibition design. With the Colorado House, ARO have proved that their highly contextual, research-led approach – which emphasizes innovation and originality – applies equally well to regions as rural as Telluride. Here the landscape context has inspired a building on a large scale (929 square metres/10,000 square feet) but with a considerate and almost demure approach to its environs. The landscape is all – it is the reason for being here – and the house reflects and respects that fact.

left The hallway to the rear of the house leads directly to the open-plan kitchen and breakfast/dining room. The floor plan allows for a choice of three dining areas, including a courtyard.

above The bedrooms benefit from individually oriented panoramas. Each bedroom was designed around a particular aspect of the landscape and planned accordingly.

MOUNTAIN GUEST HOUSE
MACK SCOGIN MERRILL ELAM, Dillard, Georgia, USA 2001

An enigmatic echo of the architects' design for their clients' original house nearby, the Mountain Guest House is also an entity in its own right. Combining a garage/store with a self-contained lodge, plus terrace and suspended deck, the house is layered with contradictions between solidity and transparency, drama and concealment. Set within a grove of poplars, it is a house hidden purposefully in the tree line.

The houses of Mack Scogin and Merrill Elam are determinedly contemporary structures, juxtaposing old and new materials and structural themes, but with the congregational nature of old farmsteads, with their traditional collections of interconnected barns, outbuildings, silos and living quarters. Mack Scogin Merrill Elam's houses take this compound idea

to a more abstract plane: these are homes that don't reveal themselves in an instant, that offer a journey between adjoining spaces with their own formal and thematic identity, a journey between interior and exterior rooms, a dialogue between open-plan areas and more intimate, enclosed retreats. They are a world away from the pure box-like homes of Philip Johnson or Marcel Breuer, delighting in complexity, ambiguity and visual experimentation, teasing and confusing the eye.

This is certainly true of the Mountain Guest House, set within a wealth of slim poplars on a 9.7-hectare (24-acre) site in the Appalachian foothills of northern Georgia, two hours' drive north of Atlanta. Indeed, when one first looks at the building it is hard to decide exactly what is going on. A glass box bedroom appears suspended in mid-air, floating

left The bedroom is essentially a raised glass box looking across the woods and toward the owner's main house. The impression is of floating elevation or of sleeping within the tree line.

below The poplars around the building form a backdrop and visual cage, blurring the building into the landscape. This idea is accentuated further by the bamboo planting, which grows up beneath and through the walkway terrace to the left.

above an indeterminate concrete structure. To the other side of the building a walkway seems to magically project outward into the trees but comes to a full stop. The trees seem to surround much of the building like a cage, dissolving the boundaries of the structure within the woodland canopy.

The house is, in fact, composed of three basic elements: a garage and store room, a bedroom/bathroom and a raised terrace. Naturally the garage is at ground level, with concrete walls and entrance way, plus one large window. In essence, the garage is entirely subservient to the glass room above, which cantilevers out over the entrance way to the store. The garage becomes a plinth and support for the living space above – accessed by a steep ramp, introducing a diagonal to contrast with the rectangular format of the house – and the base for its adjoining slate-floored terrace, which spurs outward in the opposite direction to the ramp to become a raised walkway or viewing platform, supported by a series of stilts. The stilts disappear in the tree trunks, with the picture blurred further by bamboo planted below the walkway and growing up into it and through it via a series of lattices. No wonder the building is sometimes nicknamed 'the treehouse'.

right At dusk and night, the raised glass bedroom assumes a level of surrealism – a 'tree house' sitting among the poplars. The accommodation is accessed via the diagonal ramp to the rear of the garage entrance.

upper floor plan

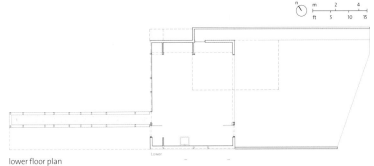

lower floor plan

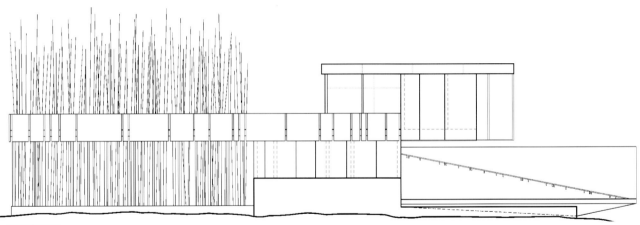

south elevation

'The trees provide a filtered privacy and help wed the house to the terrain,' says Merrill Elam. 'On the south side the poplars help shade the house in summer and allow sunlight through in winter. They also filter a view of the meadow nearby, but do not obscure it.'

The building is a satellite to the original house, by the same architects, some 50 metres (150 feet) away, which is set slightly lower into the site. Designed and built a number of years earlier for clients who wanted a vacation house that would one day become a primary residence, the main building adopts much of the same language as that which informs the guest house. Again, the low-slung, flat-roofed, single-storey building is divided into a number of components, with the main house complemented by another guest area and garage and a large, screened porch. And again, there are a number of visual games afoot, with the scale of the building unclear.

The site itself had been cleared and farmed earlier in the twentieth century, so the poplars represented relatively new growth. But with both buildings, everything possible was done to respect and preserve the landscape, with the houses woven into the existing terrain. 'Sensitivity to the landscape is a statement,' Merrill Elam says. 'In this case, it reflected the attitudes of the owners toward the stewardship of the site.'

When the client's family extended with the arrival of grandchildren, the original garage became a playroom and sleeping space began to appear limited. Hence the need for the new guest house, which offers a sense of seclusion and quiet, but with a stylistic link to the main house, which can be seen – along with the woodlands – from that glazed sleeping box.

Here, then, concealment and subversion were interrelated themes explored within the design of a building that on one level is extremely simple and on another, particularly complex. Much has been made of the practice's sensitivity to context and respect for the landscape, tying them into a tradition of sensitive modernity pioneered by the likes of Frank Lloyd Wright. Mack Scogin Merrill Elam continue to prove that such sensitivity doesn't impose limitations upon imagination or innovative creativity.

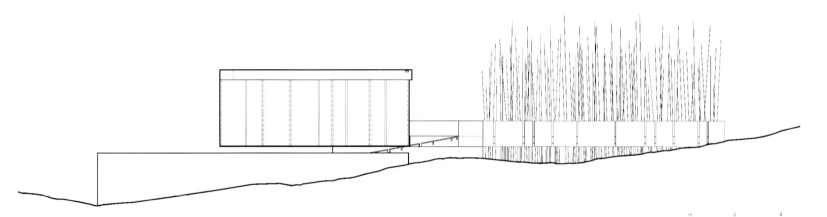

north elevation

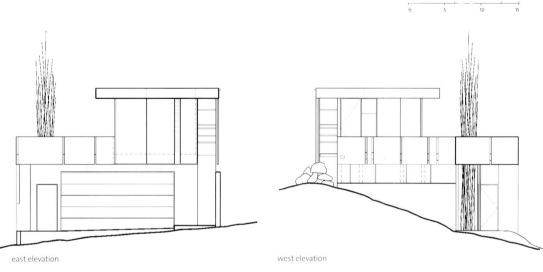

east elevation

west elevation

left The slate-covered terrace adjoining the living space gives way to the pier head projecting out into the trees. To the right of the pier head, bamboo planting emerges from slats in the structure, forming a wave of greenery.

right The entry ramp emerges up toward the rear of the living space, which is protected by a wall of translucent, frosted glass, which also provides privacy for the bathroom.

ALEX + MASÉ HOUSE

JESÚS IRISARRI & GUADALUPE PINERA, Gondomar, Pontevedra, Spain 2001

Situated at the brow of a hill in gently rolling countryside near Pontevedra in north-western Spain, not far from the Portuguese border, this ground-hugging house incorporates a multitude of ideas and references in a small space. Its apparent simplicity belies a careful but fluid design, which balances privacy and transparency, enclosed spaces and outside rooms.

If only more bungalows looked like this! More imagination and thought has gone into this small Pontevedra House by Jesús Irisarri and Guadalupe Pinera than a thousand of its predictable contemporaries. It answers the central question of how to relate to the surrounding landscape by nestling within it and connecting to it, but has many more tricks up its sleeve than most conventional single-storey houses.

Essentially the house is a large rectangle, with private spaces to the rear and more open, public parts of the house to the front, facing south and looking out across the green landscape of rolling wooded hills. The main living areas of the house were designed as a largely continuous, fluid space arranged

left A perforated concrete wall partially encloses the approach to the house, creating a more private entry point and offering a cradling arm to bathroom, kitchen and hallway on this side of the house.

below The façade of the house offers a sequence of contrasts between translucence and solidity, as well as between materials. Here the doors to the central veranda stand open.

around a central patio, without corridors or wasted space. This small courtyard garden – the contemporary equivalent or reinvention of a traditional device, especially across Spain and North Africa – is bordered by sliding and folding glass doors and acts as light source and ventilator, as well as promoting the sense of connection between outdoors and in. It becomes an ambiguous space, an integral part of the house in summer – when salvers of water are placed on the ground to help cool the home and throw out reflections – and a glazed central tank of light in winter.

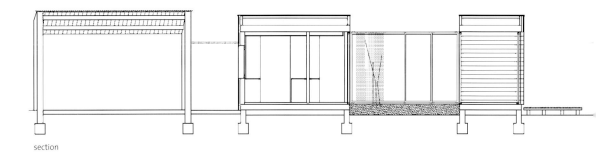

section

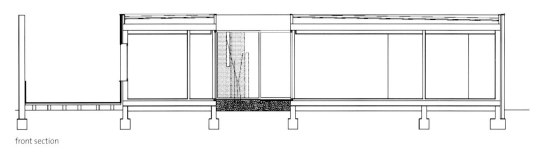

left The modest courtyard garden at the centre of the house, with its pebbles and timber and young bamboo, acts as a light well for the house and a ventilator, as well as dissolving boundaries between outdoors and in.

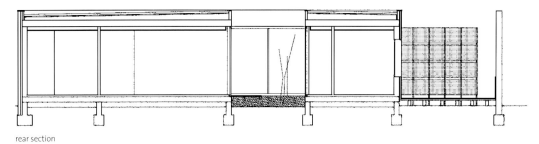

front section

The veranda to the front of the house also has an enigmatic quality, with a wealth of permutations. Two sequences of sliding and folding doors – one in glass (internal) and one largely in polycarbon (external) – create a highly flexible space, which allows a gradation of spatial experiences from complete openness to the landscape and grounds, to a more accentuated filtering of light and a greater sense of separation. Thus the house moves through varying degrees of translucence, shifting from open belvedere to a more sheltered, enclosed and cradling space. Irisarri explains:

We began designing the house in quite an abstract way, looking at the idea of one large, continuous space formed from various different elements and enclosures, with the capacity to change and mutate in many different ways. It gives the owners many different levels on which to live with nature and it's very important that the house changes through and with the seasons.

The use of relatively raw, industrial materials – from the polished concrete floors to the polycarbon panels – represents the practice's ongoing interest in exploring the application of a more unusual, experimental – and affordable – palette of tones and textures within a domestic context. Their renovation of the Segade House in Fragosela, near Vigo in north-west Spain, for instance, juxtaposed the stone exterior of the original building with a new wing clad in boards made of a cement and wood-fibre mix, which, again, are more usually applied in commercial or industrial situations.

Yet this relative rawness is mitigated and

rear section

left The sequence of sliding and folding doors to either side of the veranda allows a series of possibilities and permutations, closing up or opening out the house to the landscape.

right With both sequences of veranda doors opened out, the main living areas of the house connect directly to the meadows and forestry, maximizing the sense of a belvedere.

softened by the use of more natural, organic elements, such as stone in the patio and the pine cladding that coats one end of the house containing the reception area, kitchen and – to the rear – bathroom. This part of the house is partially protected and enclosed by a curving, monolithic concrete wall at one remove from the main house, which creates a semi-private terrace and approach. At the opposite end of the house, a study can be easily opened up to main living spaces or closed in with sliding doors.

The orientation of the house maximizes the view from the central living spaces out across minimally landscaped grassland and the woodland of the surrounding countryside. In good weather, the house effectively unfolds and opens itself to the landscape,

becoming a pavilion that frames the view and the horizon, while the low-slung nature of the building makes it unobtrusive and sympathetic to the beauty of the undulating Galician hills.

With all of its folding panels and sliding doors, the Alex + Masé house is something of a Chinese puzzle, and all the more entertaining and light-hearted for it. The focus on flexibility and multi-functionality, as well as relatively low-cost materials and construction, creates a model for a contemporary reinterpretation of the Miesian translucent box as a more complex, adaptable, and in many ways more rewarding home, which allows for privacy as well as exposure, for intimacy as well as pastoral poetry.

BERMAN HOUSE
HARRY SEIDLER & ASSOCIATES, Joadja, New South Wales, Australia 1999

Perched on a remote clifftop location in the Southern Highlands of New South Wales, the Berman House is a vibrant statement building. It is also an innovative structure – with its wave-shaped roof and cantilevered façade and balcony – as well as a largely self-sufficient home, with rainwater collection and solar cells. And it is anchored to its site by organic sandstone base walls, juxtaposed with the modernity of steel and glass.

Initially Australia, for Harry Seidler, was not a great attraction – he had to be persuaded by his family to come. But it soon proved a liberating experience, as he began to build and expand upon the treasured precepts of Modernism, looking to create an architecture that suited this new context and always exploring the opportunities offered by advances in engineering and the technology of materials. Seidler has become Australia's erudite architectural professor: much of his work is focused on its cities and suburbs, where he has built a portfolio of apartment buildings, high rises and homes, although his work has also carried him to Europe, America and Asia. And in the countryside, he has created a number of powerful one-off houses, such as the Berman House in New South Wales.

left Seen from below, the drama of the cantilevered steel-framed terrace becomes very apparent. The house perches on the edge of the cliff face, maximizing the view and challenging gravity.

The house appears to teeter dramatically on the edge of a high cliff face, with woodland and river down in the valley far below. It has a sculptural pair of wave-like roofs or canopies, which splash over the edges of the building to either side, helping to demarcate two distinct but adjacent sections of the building on two floor levels, with an additional basement space beneath. To the front of the building, overlooking the cliff, is a sky-deck living room with glass walls to three sides, creating the impression that the space is floating above and within the landscape with the undulating brush and tree line all around. Toward the rear of the living room, a monolithic slab-stone fireplace helps determine a dining area, without forming a solid dividing wall across the width of the overall space. And to one side the room flows out onto a terrace and projecting balcony, which cantilevers outward on a bed of steel. Here one can sit and relax, suspended in the void above the deep valley floor.

The second, rectangular platform of the house lies further back and parallel to the cliff, connecting with the sky deck to form an L-shaped plan for the building. Bedrooms, bathrooms and kitchen are all located in this more cellular section of the house. To one side is a landward terrace, with an ornamental pool below a highly textured wall of local sandstone. A swimming pool is set slightly apart from the main house, positioned between two large outcrops of rock, which help structure the pool walls.

On the one hand, the house – with its own cantilevered glass pavilion pushing outward from, and leaving behind, the rest of the house – is ultra-modern and rather 'James Bond', reminiscent of some of the futuristic, gravity-defying houses of John Lautner as well as Philip Johnson's House on Lloyds Neck, Long Island, New York. There is perhaps, too, an echo of the sculpted forms of Oscar Niemeyer, with whom Seidler once worked, briefly, in Brazil. In this remote, virgin locale, Seidler pushes the boundaries with the curving white-painted, steel-framed and coated roof – recalling earlier wave experiments, such as his Pittwater House – as well as the engineering of the projecting elements of the house.

But the house is also energy and resource efficient. With a lack of mains water, rain is collected

left The sky-court living room maximizes the sense of transparency and light, becoming a glass pavilion floating in the landscape. The stone fireplace creates a partial divider to the dining area.

far right Seen from above, the L-shaped formation of the house becomes apparent, as well as the curvilinear forms of the twin wave roofs. Steel piloti supports help anchor the front of the building.

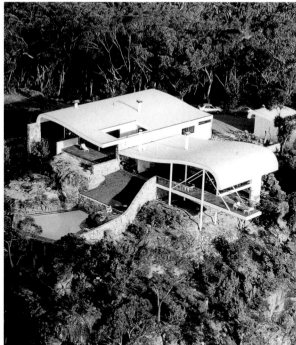

section

site plan

from the roof and stored in large tanks underneath the house, while waste is chemically treated in situ and then used for irrigation. The pool water is solar heated and can be pumped to sprinklers around the building, from where it can be used to help fight threatening bush fires. Materials have also been selected for their fireproof qualities, with concrete floors plus block and stone walls, as well as sandstone retaining walls and support piers, which help bond the house to the site literally and visually.

Set within a powerful context, the house is cited as an example of Seidler's enduring love of a 'Heroic' Modernist style. But with its focus on sustainability and self-sufficiency and its natural defence system against the real danger of forest fires, it is also a house that has a pragmatic level of bucolic common sense and green logic. And it is a home directly and forcefully connected to the landscape: here, statement architecture seeks to enhance the experience of the site itself and to live up to the drama of the clifftop backdrop.

left The master bedroom benefits from views to the rear of the house through the glass curtain walls. The sense of connection with the exterior is reinforced by the adjoining terraces.

below left The varying uses of stone for floors and certain walls helps link the house to the rocky site and offers an organic sensibility that contrasts with the high drama of the steel and glass.

right The cantilevered terrace projects out into the void above the valley and river far below. The experience is enriched and dramatized further by the use of glass for the balustrade.

JACOB'S LADDER
NIALL MCLAUGHLIN, Oxfordshire, UK 2002

The main impetus behind the design of Jacob's Ladder – set within a plateau clearing on a four-hectare (ten-acre) woodland site on an Oxfordshire hillside – was the inspirational vistas and setting. With a nod to Mies van der Rohe, this lightweight, eco-conscious home is among a limited number of truly innovative English rural houses from recent years keeping alive the long tradition of the individual country house in the British landscape.

For Niall McLaughlin, issues such as sustainability, context, light and the inventive use of materials and tectonic technology are more important than establishing a clear-cut style or regular aesthetic. His frame of reference is broad, his concerns and interests varied, and his projects so different from one another than it's difficult to detect the hand of the author. His

attention-grabbing Photographer's Shack of 1996, for instance, was a zoomorphic lakeside retreat that looked like a prehistoric bird struggling to take flight. It is a world away from Jacob's Ladder, an Oxfordshire country house that owes more to the Californian Case Study Houses of Charles and Ray Eames and associates than to the aviary.

The site for Jacob's Ladder is a clearing in a wooded hillside, with striking views out across the Oxfordshire landscape. The clients, photographer David Grey and his wife Shelley, took down a rambling house on the site in order to replace it with something contemporary and free flowing, tied to the surroundings. They wanted a fluid design, with little in the way of doors, barriers or solid divisions, preferring the idea of inter-linked spaces with constant connections between one another and from

left A series of terraces and verandas to both levels of the house reinforces the relationship between interiors and exterior. It is a house that opens itself outward in the summer.

right The house sits within a clearing in the woods, facing outward from its hillside position toward the rolling Oxfordshire countryside beyond a gap in the surrounding trees.

inside to out. McLaughlin explains his solution to his clients' brief:

They asked for our building to be a frame from which they could experience the wood and that idea of a building as a frame rather than an object is very attractive. The house is designed to help you experience the landscape and by using glass in the major rooms we are suggesting that the edge of the trees in the clearing constitutes the real edge of the house. In the future we hope that the house and the wood will become increasingly intertwined.

A key reference point became a visit McLaughlin had undertaken to Mies van der Rohe's Tugendhat House in Brno, Czech Republic, which Mies completed in 1930 – the same year he became head of the Bauhaus. Tugendhat is a large building on a sloping site on the outskirts of the city facing south toward park land and McLaughlin was interested in the way people moving through the house would constantly catch glimpses of the vista beyond. The house is accessed from the rear, via its upper level, so that you descend downward to the main living room with its vast wall of glass opening out to the parkland view, forming what has been described as a belvedere within the main body of the house.

Although Jacob's Ladder is a more modestly sized and far more lightweight structure, made with a steel frame, timber cladding and a wealth of glass, there are similarities with Tugendhat. Here, too, you enter the building from the rear and into the upper level, via a bridge that flows from a pathway emerging from the trees. Here, too, you descend to the main living room – a dramatic double-height space – where sheets of glass lead you out to the Oxfordshire landscape, which unfolds before you through a gap in the tree line. This pivotal view is glimpsed as you journey through the house and becomes a focus on the trip down the cylindrical staircase, where you look out to a water feature on the roof of the projecting swimming pool pavilion below. The rectangular pool, which is charcoal-lined, provides an opportunity to swim out from the house and into the landscape.

A series of decks and terraces – as well as the use of a cantilevered flat roofline, projecting canopy-like beyond the main living spaces – reinforces the sense

left The swimming pool projects outward from the front of the house, like a waterway heading into the view. The idea is to create the sensation of swimming out into the landscape.

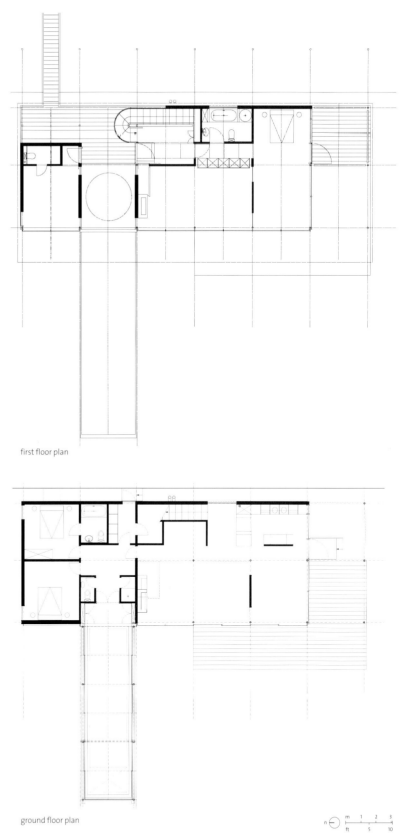

first floor plan

ground floor plan

section

m 1 2 3
ft 5 10

of a light, semi transparent structure and further dissolves the boundaries between indoors and out. Indeed, for McLaughlin, it's essential that a country house, in particular, is fully integrated into its environment. Here, the impact on the site itself was minimal: the 45 beech trees felled to make the cutaway opening in the forest to the view beyond were used for decks and flooring within and around the house. Glazing incorporates toughened, double-glazed and low emissivity panels to preserve energy, filtering light in the summer months and insulating the building at colder times of the year.

Jacob's Ladder will no doubt be among the first of a series of environmentally friendly houses and buildings from McLaughlin. For this part of the world, the house is a radical step. Within the broader context of seeking solutions to questions related to new-build sustainability and site sensitivity it seems as logical and aesthetically pleasing a solution as one might hope to find. It will be fascinating to see where McLaughlin goes from here.

left The double-height living room is the heart of the house and has a precious sense of scale and drama. The soaring curtain wall creates a strong sense of transparency in this part of the house.

right The master bedroom is a large enough space to also serve as a sitting room, from where to enjoy the view. It also adjoins the raised terrace, which serves as a complementary outdoor room.

OBERWALDER/KUTSCHA HOUSE
BÜRO KO A LA, Graz, Austria 2003

With a fusion team of architect and landscape designer, the young Austrian practice Büro Ko a la has developed a distinctive approach to landscape design and planning with projects that look to dissolve the boundaries between buildings and natural surroundings. Extending their portfolio, the practice has now also created a unique house near Graz that draws on the same principles.

It appears that we might be moving once again from an era of high specialization toward a more renaissance spirit – championed by the pioneer modernists – where disciplines begin to blur and the

walls erected between distinct professions start to crumble. The benefits of crossing borders and creative interdisciplinary partnerships can be seen in the work of Austrian practice Büro Ko a la, formed at the turn of the new century by landscape planner Robert Kutscha and architect Veronika Oberwalder.

Both had been involved in running their own farm for a number of years before opening their practice, based in Graz, and personally are drawn to rural landscapes and contexts, although their work has addressed urban projects as well as bucolic challenges. And for themselves, the two have created a new home on the edge of a largely agricultural

left The front section of the house opens out to the meadow and valley lands beyond. This part of the house, holding the main living space, is largely fluid and open plan.

right The stone wall, which borders parts of the house, including the satellite building to one side, forms an organic root to the land, while the glazed façade allows the landscape in.

village to the east of Graz, a house bound into the landscape. They have purposefully blurred the edges of where their intervention begins and ends, establishing radiant connections between outside and in and creating a house that should lead to further explorations of the territory where landscape and architecture intertwine. Kutscha explains:

We do try to place buildings and the surrounding landscape in a relationship with one another. It's important for us that architecture and designed landscape react to each other. That doesn't mean that a house should disappear.... The architecture should be absolutely apparent but distinctive and valid, reacting to local conditions, typologically, functionally, formally, materially and socially.

Their own slim, long, rectangular, single-storey home, then, is pushed into its hillside site, looking down and across meadowlands, with views out to the Styrian hills. The roof of the building has been grassed over, so in some senses, when seen from the village and access road further up the hillside, the house seems to become a part of the meadow itself, almost submerged within the face of the hill. The structure of the building has been split into a small number of constituent parts, with the main body of the concrete-framed house divided in two.

left The stone retaining wall wraps the back of the house in an organic coat This is the largely closed aspect, toward the nearby road, with a thin strip of glazing to the rear rooms.

above The architects made an arrangement with local farmers to plant the uncultivated field in front of the house as they wish. In summer it becomes a flower-filled meadow.

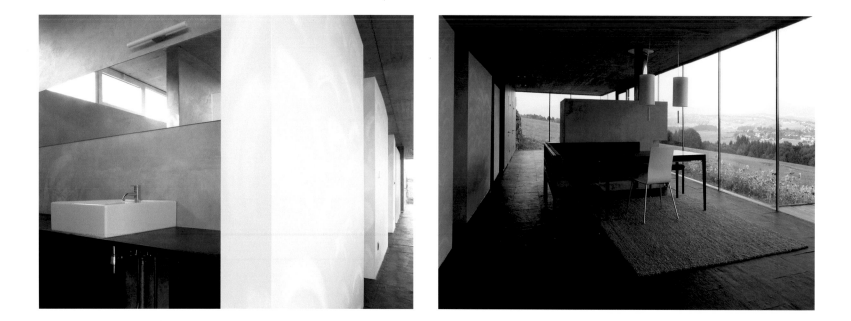

The front section of the main house, overlooking the meadow, is a largely open-plan living and dining area – together with a freestanding, slim and compact kitchen – with glazing to three sides creating a high level of transparency and inviting the panoramic landscape into the heart of the house. Facing north-east, the glazing does not overheat the house, nor is there a need for protective curtains or blinds. A monolithic fireplace slab, with the roof in untreated concrete and the floors in black slate, helps to partially divide the space into zones for relaxation and dining.

Beyond this open part of the house lies a stretch of more intimate spaces reaching back into the rear and to the enclosed, faceless side of the house – only a simple strip of glazing allows light to percolate through. Within this block sit an entrance hall, a number of more functional spaces, study and two bedrooms – timber-lined escapes, using zebrano wood, with a more organic aesthetic. Indeed the materials throughout juxtapose natural materials like timber and slate with more synthetic elements, such as concrete, glass and steel. All have a raw simplicity but contrasting textures and finishes.

Terraces lie to one side of the house – outdoor rooms on a level with the main living space – while to the other, a small courtyard divides the main building

from a small satellite unit for services and storage. Dry-stone basalt walls form a kind of wrap around parts of the building, enclosing the rear of the main house and then folding round to enclose the front section of the satellite. This wall, like the grass roof, helps mitigate the more extreme and exposed elements of the house, while also being an essential part of the modest landscaping around the perimeters of the building. 'We tried to design a radically contemporary building but then inserted it into the slope, like a change of level', says Kutscha. 'It was an act of reverence to the rural surroundings.'

In many ways the house is a minimal structure, with little in the way of embellishment. Yet given the methods used to connect the house to the landscape, together with the use of tactile surfaces and subtle material shifts, the building avoids any of the soulless paucity often associated with minimal interiors. Indeed, here the landscape becomes a key wall of the house, a wall with all the colours and constantly shifting patterns of the seasons and the passing hours of the day and night.

far left Bathrooms and bedrooms lie to the more private rear section of the building, aligned in a regular, cellular formation, with strip glazing to the back of the house.

left The glass façade of the house allows the landscape to flood into the main living space. The meadows are planted with wild flowers by arrangement with local farmers.

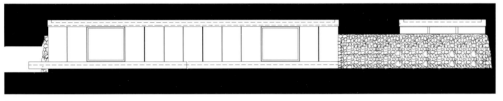

front elevation

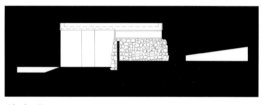

side elevation

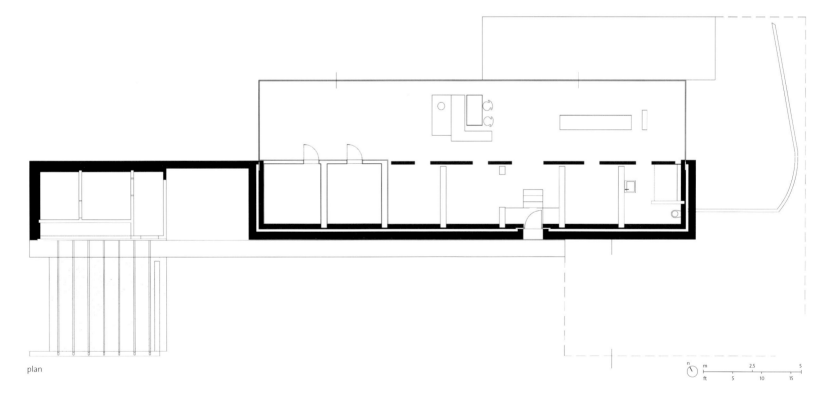

plan

LA CASA
ELIZABETH WRIGHT INGRAHAM, Colorado Springs, Colorado, USA 1996

Perched atop a Colorado cliff, with a dramatic projecting skywalk reaching out into thin air, La Casa is a bold intervention in an extreme, photographic setting. Situated within unlandscaped scrub, the house appears incongruous and surreal, yet is carefully oriented around the endless vistas and designed with a focus on sustainability and environmental awareness.

With its isolated clifftop position, Elizabeth Wright Ingraham's La Casa is reminiscent, in some respects, of a fortress or *castello*. Like a fortress, it adopts a defensive, strategic position within the landscape, raised and exposed for high visibility. But this defiant composition is also protected by virtue of its

commanding, seemingly untouchable position. It expresses an understanding, a respect for the natural environment, which is inevitably part of its reason for being, yet one cannot help see within it a triumph over nature and a solid, immovable structure, which exists against the odds and the elements.

Alternatively, one can see La Casa as a beacon or a landlocked lighthouse, or a grand belvedere, but it is still very much an intervention upon the locale. The drama of the landscape lends gravitas and power to the house, which might in other contexts be a far more obscure building. Like Adalberto Libera's Casa Malaparte, that solitary home on the cliffs of Capri, or even Fallingwater – the iconic achievement of Wright Ingraham's grandfather – La Casa is emboldened,

below A guest satellite sits off to one side of the main building, which is set among the arid desert scrub. The surrounding site is being returned to its preconstruction raw and natural state.

right The dramatic, cantilevered steel skywalk, which floats above the desert wilderness below, was a response to the need to set the house some way back from the potentially unstable cliff face.

below Being physicians, who might be called out at all times and in all weathers, the clients requested a glass block walkway to connect the main house to the garaging and cars.

right Perched above the valley, the house could almost be read as an additional layering of the cliff, whose rows of limestone and sandstone deposits step downward to the desert below.

enhanced, enriched and inspired by the way it sits within and reacts to an extraordinary position in the natural world.

The 465-square-metre (5000-square-foot) house – designed for two physicians – is set within a 1.2-hectare (3-acre) site not far from Colorado Springs. The rocky position has the drop of the 46-metre (150-foot) limestone/sandstone cliff to the south, a ravine to the north and the city and mountains to the east and to the west. The erosion and instability of the cliff edge encouraged Wright Ingraham to place the house at a slight remove, so as to anchor it more firmly to its limestone base. But to make up for this small compromise, the house features a 'skywalk', which projects out of the front of the building into the void, rather like the glass balcony in Harry Seidler's Berman House in Australia (see pages 124–9). As Wright Ingraham explains:

The client's programme, which drove the design, was the need for privacy, safety, views, natural daylight, easy maintenance and easy movement. While some of these requirements posed contradictions we managed

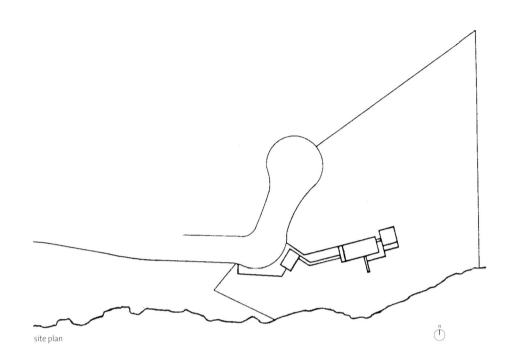

site plan

left and far left The interiors are oriented around a double-height living room, with ample glazing to the panoramas beyond. Materials are intentionally raw and simple for low maintenance and to showcase the client's art collection.

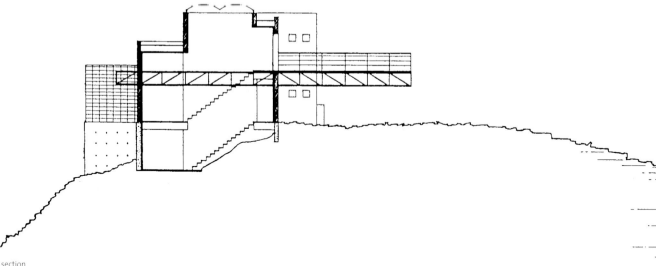

section

to arrange the rectangular forms so that there was
bright natural light in all rooms with good privacy
without any window or door coverings. The skywalk
was a response to the unstable cliffs and a place where
one could stand and capture the splendid views
without enclosure and with safety.[1]

The skywalk is complemented by a raised terrace,
which also looks out across this mesmeric panorama
and sits above a pair of study rooms below it.

The concrete block walls, the high epic glazing
and heated floors help mitigate the extreme
temperature shifts and climatic extremes that assault
the house. Indeed, the potential hostility of the
environment – with its heat, cold and high winds –
was another determining factor in the choice of
materials and the evolution of the design, as well as
the request for a low-maintenance structure. There is
even a glass-block walkway connecting the garage to
the house to enclose the owners on harsh days as
they head to their cars.

The floor plan of the house involved the creation
of a double-height living space, with its own small
terrace, with the master suite situated above the
kitchen and dining room. To the rear of the master
bedroom there is a bank of glazing offering views to
the north, as well as the glazing to the southern

sweep. The protruding skywalk is accessed from this
upper level and becomes an extension of the stairwell
and landing. An interconnected guest wing is set off
to one side of the house, offering an independent co-
existence to visitors.

The interiors soften the overall atmosphere of
the house, with organic terracotta tiles in key living
spaces, while the walls have a purposeful neutrality to
best display the client's art collection. Glazing is in
low-emissivity thermal glass and much of the
rainwater is recycled, fitting in with Elizabeth Wright
Ingraham's continuing emphasis on sustainability,
treating the land 'as a resource, not a commodity'.[2]

La Casa, indeed, unites many of the themes that
have long interested Wright Ingraham: sustainability,
contextuality, orientation in terms of landscape and
light, block construction. She has been labelled a
'maverick', an independently minded voice setting her
own agenda. La Casa – an original window onto a
natural wonder played out on an epic scale – suggests
she still has much to say.

[1] Elizabeth Wright Ingraham, briefing notes on La Casa

[2] Elizabeth Wright Ingraham website (www.ewrightingraham.com)

MARTE SINGLE FAMILY HOUSE
MARTE & MARTE, Dafins, Vorarlberg, Austria 1999

Built into the banks of a heavily sloping hillside site, overlooking the Rhine Valley, the house Stefan Marte built for himself and his family was a direct response to this challenging but mesmeric location. A concrete frame and shell building, it pushes itself into the topography, creating a striking contrast between its own artificiality and the concept of concealment.

The work of Marte & Marte is about clarity and purity of form. Their houses, especially, strip away superfluous detailing and ornament, seeking an original building free of obvious stylistic and architectural references. They are interested in homes that form a dialogue with surroundings and occupants. In particular, this dialogue has meant exploring the familiar dialectic between translucence and enclosure in frank and original ways, while also looking to provide breaks in the clearly defined forms and lines of their designs to allow key spaces to flow outward into the land.

With their Holiday Home in Furx of 2001 – an isolated mountaintop house clad in larch – for instance, the design revolved around four large areas of glazing, which pierce the house and frame panoramic vistas of Lake Constance and the surrounding mountains. Marte & Marte describe these four openings as lenses, with varying methods of exposure, while key living spaces revolve around these essential views.

The same is true, in many respects, of Stefan Marte's own home, which frames and celebrates striking views of the Rhine Valley, but also has to adapt to a far more challenging topography, built directly into the steep hillside slope on the outskirts of the small village of Dafins. The new house, like the existing buildings in the village, closely follows the course of the winding road running through the community. But unlike the traditional Alpine homes and nineteenth-century farmhouses in the area, the concrete-shelled building is a house of obvious and purposeful modernity. Marte & Marte were interested in the relationship established between these two simply detailed building types, the old and the new, yet the site itself was the essential driving force behind the architecture of their house. As Stefan Marte explains:

The house is a completely new interpretation of a building in a rural setting, and the initial inspiration was the steep slope. It resulted in a concept that could

left The new house follows the line of the winding mountain road that runs through the village. It stands in stark contrast to the traditional, alpine timber houses nearby.

right The side of the building is largely faceless, with a mass of concrete slabs. The house is oriented to the front, with glazing on both levels soaking in the mountain views.

not be built everywhere – it was a prototype for this kind of location, with all its strengths and weaknesses. The house stands absolutely naturally in the landscape and seems to grow – without a clear starting point – out of the deep green of the meadow, as though it had always been a part of this beautiful setting.

With its closed back to the street and its transparent glazed façade pointing down and across the valley, the house sits on a base and basement section thrust back into the hill, with two floors above coated in reinforced concrete shells, which also largely close off the side of the structure. The lower floor houses the bedrooms, with the master bedroom to the front with a glazed panorama, and bathroom to the rear. The upper floor, which also acts as entrance level from the street, is split into three irregular sections: a rectangular kitchen/dining room, pushing right out to the front of the building, and a cube-shaped living room with a large roof terrace – or outdoor room – forward of it, heading toward the lip of the building.

left The kitchen/dining space – or family room – sits to the left and the separate and more private living room to the right. Between the two runs an access way to the roof terrace.

right The family room pushes right to the front of the building, with a vast picture window looking down the hillside slope. Bedrooms are situated below, with services to the rear.

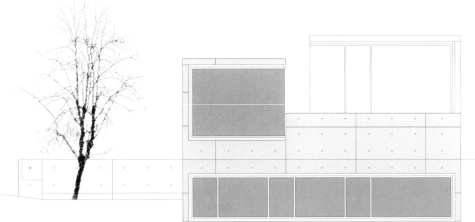

south elevation

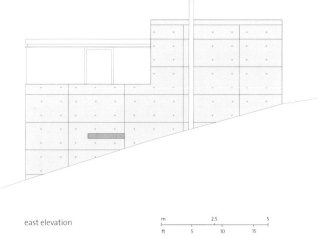

east elevation

m		2.5		5
ft	5	10	15	

north elevation

west elevation

| m | | 2.5 | | 5 |
| ft | 5 | 10 | 15 | |

151

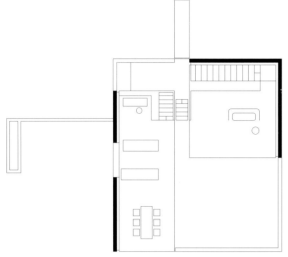

upper level floor plan

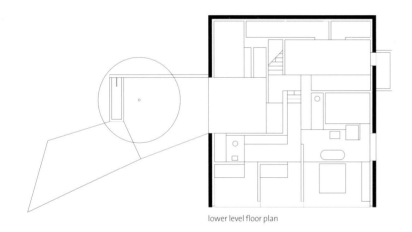

lower level floor plan

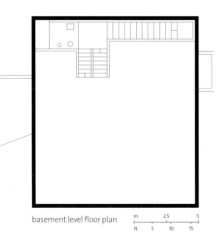

basement level floor plan

m	2.5		5
ft	5	10	15

The kitchen/diner becomes a communal, family living space. The lounge, set apart and at a slight remove – with a walkway to the terrace between it and the kitchen block – becomes a more private, contemplative escape. Yet both units have curtain windows overlooking the valley beyond, as well as glazed side walls, so that they become semi-transparent boxes interacting with one another, and together form a strong contrast with the solidity and mass of the exterior framework of the overall building. 'The really fantastic thing about this arrangement is that even when you are separate, spatially, you are still connected by the view between these two rooms', says Stefan Marte. 'When night falls, both rooms acquire a glow, an aura that is generated between the two glass constructions.'

The excitement of this building, then, lies in the vibrancy of the contradictions contained within it: the exploration of earthbound submergence juxtaposed with naked concrete artifice; the sense of openness and transparency contrasted with the solidity and powerful sense of mass, which the building can also convey. As Stefan Marte explains, in Vorarlberg the tradition of building one's own house is very strong and important. Marte's own home is an example of what he calls 'Vorarlberg international style' rather than modern vernacular. It is a powerful prototype for a new kind of mountain home.

right The kitchen and dining room form the main communal area for the family, with a stairway and entrance hall to the rear. Side glazing connects the room to the roof terrace alongside.

SHEEP FARM HOUSE
DENTON CORKER MARSHALL, Kyneton, Victoria, Australia 1998

An epic tilt-slab concrete wall, running horizontally across the remote landscape for over 200 metres (650 feet), presents a windbreak protector and abstract façade for a high-tech sheep farm amid rolling hills in central Victoria. To the other side of this sculptural slab, dropped into the countryside, lies a glass pavilion home, as well as machine sheds and a shearing house. Here Denton Corker Marshall have turned farmstead into art form.

We have a familiar idea of what a farmstead should look like: it's a compound of buildings, a gathering of barns, outbuildings, silos and farmhouse offering mutual protection and seeking common links with the landscape and topography. These are vernacular, organic buildings, tied to their surroundings by the use of local materials, such as timber and stone.

Denton Corker Marshall's new farmstead in a remote part of Victoria, north-west of Melbourne, dispenses with all those connotations in an instant. Their brief for a high-tech sheep farm, producing high-quality, ultra-fine wool, called for a farmhouse, a guest cottage, garages, machine sheds, shearing sheds and yards. But farmers Noel and Lyndsay Henderson had no great affinity with traditional domestic architecture or farmstead vernacular, while Denton Corker Marshall's innovative houses are known for their abstraction, surrealism and sculptural approach that abandons the traditional language of comfortable domesticity. The result is a single entity, a landscraper set within a fold in the undulating hills, hidden behind an extraordinary concrete wall, 217 metres (712 feet) long, whose rawness seems to reflect the rugged nature of the location.

This heroic landmark line denies both domesticity and farmstead imagery, creating a grey industrial slab slicing into the landscape like a lightning strike. But it is also a powerful, beautiful intervention, a new-era windbreak, a fortress sinking into the land. It has echoes of Luis Barragán, Ricardo Legoretta and other Mexican Modernists obsessed with that country's emphasis on the power of the high, monotonous wall. At Barragán's Cuadra San Cristobal (see page 14) – another farmstead – the

right The long 'breezeway' between the great holding wall and the house itself forms a porch and partially sheltered access run to the machinery shed and cottage nearby.

far right The owners of the house think of the holding wall as a rock in the landscape. It serves not just as a shelter but also as a linking device to bring the farm buildings together.

famously coloured slab walls reinvent the haciendas of the past with new, bold statements of intent. Likewise, Denton Corker Marshall have created an iconic reinterpretation of the Australian farm. As John Denton explains:

Our work tends to reject the vernacular, or at least reinterpret it in a singularly contemporary way. However, the houses do respond to their circumstances. The south-eastern Australian country house has to deal with extreme heat in summer and cold windy weather in winter. When flying over south-east Australia the pattern of farming is seen clearly with formal windbreak interventions, usually dark green cypress planting. Our initial idea was to also 'make a line' on the landscape with a concrete wall windbreak that acted as a link element for all the parts of the farm. At the same time this wall acted as the approach 'view' of the house with everything protected behind that wall.

A deep inset into the line of the wall also creates the outline of a pair of open arms with an entry courtyard within the indent. A secondary, slightly higher charcoal wall demarcates the approach to the house itself while the entrance is an oblique slash in this double skin with a yellow 'front door'.

Beyond the wall, a new world – and a new set of references – becomes apparent. There is a momentary gap between the wall and the house, which forms both 'porch' and a covered 'breezeway' running parallel to the wall, leading you around to other elements within the farmstead, particularly the machine shed and cottage to the other sides of the walled section of the courtyard. The house, meanwhile, is before you: essentially it is a glass

above The wall forms a massive courtyard entry point for the main house. The holding wall is complemented by another higher wall to the far side, denoting the main house, with a modest oblique doorway.

above right The main house is a glass pavilion – a sophisticated lean-to backing onto the holding wall. The roof line slopes beyond the curtain walls to form a veranda.

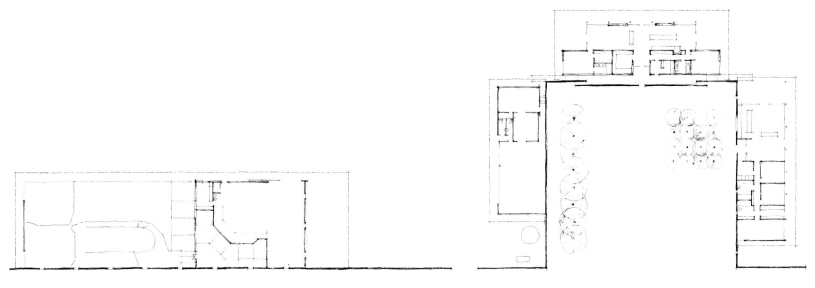

plan

pavilion with a sloping roof projecting downward and outward to the north-east with an overhang offering shade to a long veranda. Steel supports reach up from ground to ceiling, piercing the roofline. The glass façade of the house opens the building up to the landscape beyond, dissolving divisions between the two and offering panoramic views of the surrounding farmland. Within the overall glass-cased living space of the pavilion are two rather more solid box-like elements, which contain bedrooms and utility areas. The whole is united by the simplicity of materials – polished concrete floors, timber cupboards and units, stainless-steel worktops – while detailing is kept to a minimum throughout. Even elements like gutters disappear within the overall structure of the building.

The Sheep Farm House, then, becomes a place of high contrast, between the closed, more industrial face to the world and the alternative, open and glazed façade. One side of the house connects with the landscape and invites it inside, the other denies the landscape and declares its artificial intent. Yet overall, through the way the farmstead is positioned low in the contours of the site, seeking a natural degree of protection and concealment, there is at last one pragmatic echo of the traditional farmstead, which also sought comfort and a working, symbiotic relationship with the land.

right The large veranda, together with the transparent walls of the key living spaces in the pavilion, dissolves the divisions between indoors and out, with views out across the farmland and to the granite hills in the distance.

The country house has long been an engine of change and diversification. Architects are still drawn to the vibrant form of the new country home as a point of experimentation and change, a focal point for thinking about the way we live. The new country house as a stand-alone beacon of architectural and social shift has a particular resonance. It represents an opportunity to freely explore thematic, structural and formal experiments, while also addressing the continuing fascination with prototypical concept houses that can answer the demands for affordable, sustainable homes suited to a range of rural contexts. Context remains the guiding light as the new country house proves itself one of the great laboratories of architectural change.

CASA TAGOMAGO
CARLOS FERRATER, Santa Eulalia del Rio, Ibiza, Spain 2001

On a clifftop site on the north-eastern coast of Ibiza, near Santa Eulalia and overlooking the island of Tagomago, Carlos Ferrater has built a distinctive vacation house in concrete and sandstone. The house has been subdivided, with the main living spaces complemented by a number of identical, cellular pavilions for individual members of the client's family; form and materials unify the whole.

The country house has long enjoyed defying stereotypes and asking engaging questions. Why should a home conform to a standardized view of a single-unit, two-storey building, with living space down below and bedrooms upstairs? Isn't such conformity totally counterproductive when it takes no account of context or the bespoke requirements of its owners? The majority of new homes still adopt this standard, unthinking pattern, but others delight in stretching boundaries, rethinking form according to the creative logic of function and location.

This is obviously true of Carlos Ferrater's Casa Tagomago, a vacation house on the island of Ibiza, which, from some perspectives, looks little like a house at all. Divided into six units of living space, plus garaging – united by bleached sandstone façades and walkways – it has a compound, angular and geometric look. In fact, it is less reminiscent of the compound look of farmsteads or vernacular communal units than of certain contemporary hotels, where accommodation is split between various pavilions or cabins, united by common aesthetics.

One sees this kind of experimentation with cellular forms in some other notable country houses, such as Josh Sweitzer's Monument House in

below The four regular pavilions each contain a bedroom and bathroom, with large shuttered windows and individual terraces. To the far right stands a guest pavilion.

right The pavilions are concrete framed but faced with sandstone. Each has been designed so that it can be extended should a new generation demand more space.

California's Joshua Tree National Park, or Hiroshi Hara's Ito House amid a forested site near Nagasaki, Japan, which is divided into two shingle-clad living space cubes for parents and children, plus a rectangular block with additional living rooms. Here the family co-exists, coming together to share the location and communal activities, but then retreating to self-contained spaces, which offer privacy, autonomy and independence.

This is very much the idea, also, at Casa Tagomago. Here, a communal, glass-fronted pavilion cradles the kitchen and a combined living and dining room, with the client's master bedroom and services to one side. In front of this pavilion is a large timber deck or terrace – with views out across the ocean and the island of Tagomago – leading to the swimming pool. But side by side with this pavilion, within a

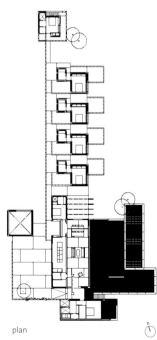

plan

rectangular, orderly formation leading one away from the terrace and pool, are four identical pavilions for the client's children, each one containing a double bedroom and a bathroom. At the end of this sequence is a guest annex, set apart and to one remove from the rest of the family's accommodation, with a rooftop sun terrace.

The overall structure is lent cohesion and unity not only through the use of repeated forms and materials – essentially concrete shells with a coat of damp-proofed sandstone – but also by a minimal aesthetic, which creates a very pure and serene building, described by Ferrater as almost monastic. The longitudinal building is also united by the common pattern of terraces and walkways – in stone, cement or timber – which contrasts markedly with the raw, unlandscaped Mediterranean surroundings of the house, with the heavy growth of pine and juniper trees.

above A large canopy or pergola forms a sheltered element to the terrace, as well as offering a filter effect for the light that streams into the main part of the house, to the right of the pool and terrace.

above right The main building block of the house is itself split into a number of sections. Fluid living space dominates the central, glass-fronted aspect of the house, while bedrooms are to the wings.

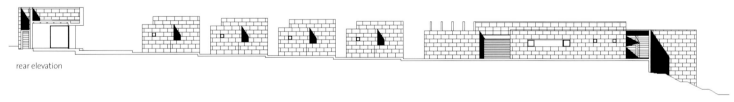

rear elevation

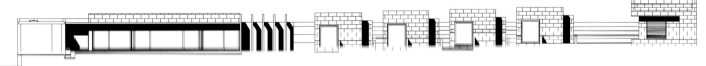

front elevation

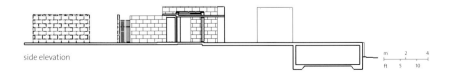

side elevation

m   2   4
ft   5   10

Casa Tagomago, then, becomes a highly flexible house, which can expand or retreat according to the number of inhabitants. The pavilions can easily be opened up or closed down, each having its own large shuttered doorway, which, when open, provides an active dialogue between inside and out. The main house, too, looks to dissolve the boundaries between interior and exterior: its glazed façade incorporates large sliding doors. The adjoining terrace is partially sheltered by a large canopy or pergola, which creates a halfway point between outside and in, offering shade and relief from the intensity of the summer sun and also helping to mitigate the effect of solar gain on the main living block behind it. Outbuildings could be extended or adapted, should the need arise, adding more flexibility to the scheme.

A prolific architect, Carlos Ferrater is known for his commercial buildings, parks and convention centres, transport hubs, hotels and apartment buildings, as well as distinctive houses. Common to his work are an interest in landscape, geometry and the qualities of the Mediterranean light, and the establishment of a particular rapport between building and environment, which he achieves partly through a sensitive sculptor's approach to materials – although he employs relatively few of them, he explores each one fully.

At Casa Tagomago, we have an exploration of the rawness of concrete allied to the more organic textures of the sandstone surfaces, partially reflecting and enjoying the distinctive quality of the diurnal patterns of light on the island site. This is set within the framework of a formal experiment that has a great sense of presence and original, geometric prowess, but also a sense of continuity with the existing architectural heritage and strong connections with this clifftop landscape.

left Large sliding glass doors open up to connect the living room to the terrace beyond, with stone flags giving way to the timber deck. The pergola frames the view outward.

right The house creates a free-flowing relationship between inside and outside spaces. The pool area and glass-fronted living room are oriented around the view out across the coast and the isle of Tagomago.

M-HOUSE
MICHAEL JANTZEN, Gorman, California, USA 2000

A pioneering concept house sited in the Tehachapi Mountains, to the north of Los Angeles, the M-House is a highly flexible, adaptable and relocatable modular eco-building from the fertile imagination of Michael Jantzen. Made up of a series of hinged panels attached to interlocking steel-framed cubes, this is a vacation house with a difference.

At the heart of Michael Jantzen's explosive geometric sculpture, known as the M-House, sit seven interlocking steel-framed cubes. These rest on platforms with adjustable legs so that the house can easily be adapted to uneven terrain. Around the

cubes, a whole series of hinged panels – made of thin sheets of a concrete composite – fold this way and that, enclosing internal living spaces, forming shutters and ceilings, doorways and windows, screens and porches, as well as folding inward to create tables and sleeping platforms. An essentially simple structure becomes a geometric experiment, a stand-alone home with echoes of lunar landers and sci-fi space colonies. It is like a space station, but one painted a pleasing, cohesive shade of green that ties in well with the rural locale of Jantzen's own prototype M-House, a hillside retreat in the Tehachapi Mountains of California. As he explains:

above Like a captivating puzzle, the M-House is formed from a series of folding panels hinged to seven interconnected steel cubes. It has no need of foundations or footings.

right The house plays with ideas of enclosure and exposure, creating halfway points such as this lobby area. The green paintwork unifies interiors and exteriors alike.

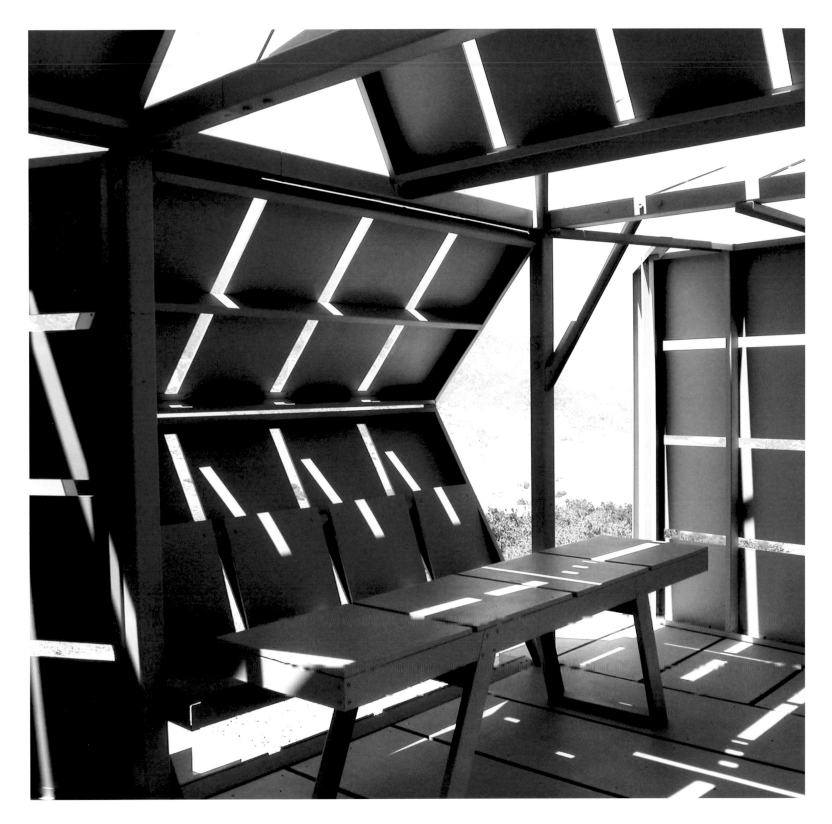

right The bed includes built-in storage underneath and sits on castors so that the whole thing can be rolled out onto the adjoining deck on warm nights for star gazing.

far right The study faces south with a built-in desk looking out across the panorama. The large pot, and some other pieces in the house, was made by the architect's wife, Ellen.

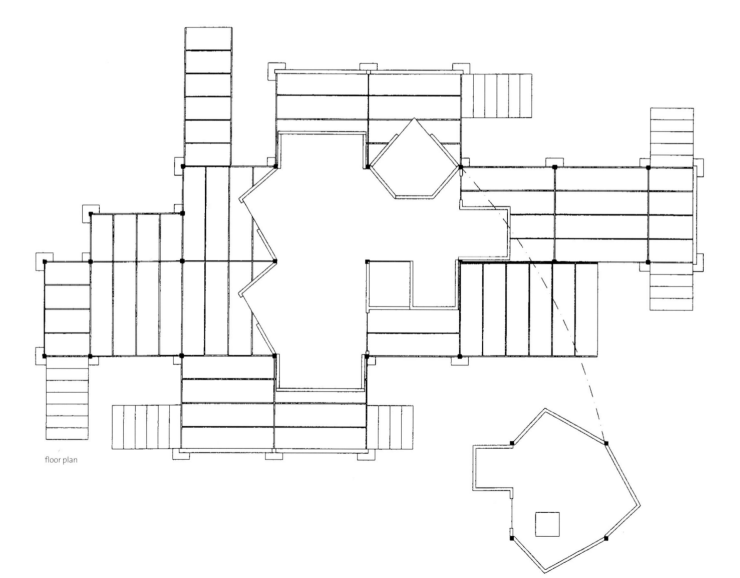

floor plan

I wanted the building to be about experiencing shape and form, and because the outline is very complex I decided it would be easier to enjoy it in a single colour. From a distance, the exterior looks like a grove of trees, and because there's lots of grass, the green outside flows into the green inside, making the space feel larger.[1]

Jantzen's own M-House serves as a one-bedroom studio and escape cabin, built by the architect himself. Yet the M-House has also been designed as a highly flexible, pre-fabricated 'M-vironment' that can be moulded at will with the addition of other cellular components and differing panel arrangements, lending itself to use not only as a vacation home, but also as an office, exhibition space, play house, retail space and so on. The M-House can also be constructed in different materials, could be easily shipped and readily assembled or disassembled in the space of a week and has no need of foundations.

A prefabricated, mass-produced, low-cost and environmentally aware modular housing system has long been an architectural Holy Grail. In the late 1940s and 1950s there were a number of experimental projects to launch the kind of concept house that could be mass produced and easily moved from place to place, offering both affordable vacation homes and fast accommodation for disaster relief or migrant populations. Richard Buckminster Fuller's Wichita House of 1946 – itself an evolution of his Dymaxion House – was a circular, moulded aluminium prefab house that fulfilled such criteria. Matti Suuronen's Futuro House of 1968 also looked rather like a UFO – a glass fibre bubble house, which could be flown anywhere by helicopter. (At one point it looked as though 15,000 might be built but the order was scrapped in the economic crisis of the early 1970s.) In France, Jean Prouvé explored similar territory with his prefab 'Meudon' and 'Tropical House' projects. In Britain, post-war prefabs were mass produced to

answer housing shortages, but were seen as stop-gap solutions rather than desirable homes.

Indeed, the desire for individuality, for homes that certainly do not look mass produced or off the shelf, has always damaged the prospects of such futuristic concept homes. But Jantzen's M-House does look individual, with its emphasis on artistry and sculpted form. Michael Jantzen trained in fine art, particularly sculpture, and uses model-making more than drawing or computers to develop his architectural work. For more than 30 years he has been fascinated with the possibilities of creating adaptable, affordable, flexible and environmentally aware housing systems. 'The design of the M-house

came out of a lot of other work that investigates the creation of systems that generate form', says Jantzen. 'I invent a system of components and let those components evolve into a structure that accommodates functional needs.'

Within its country context, the M-House can be shaped to suit a specific site. Jantzen's prototype frames the mountain views and its orientation picks up on the changing patterns of light and shade. The architect plans to add a satellite with solar panels and a wind turbine, and is also exploring the addition of a rainwater tank and a compost toilet. Such features serve to reinforce the green credentials of the project, which can itself be wholly recycled.

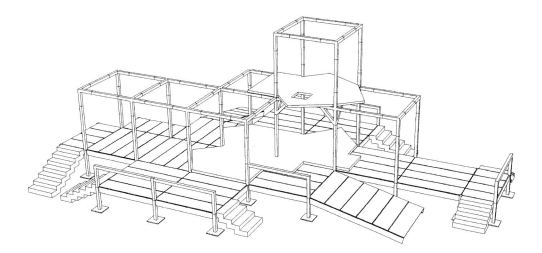

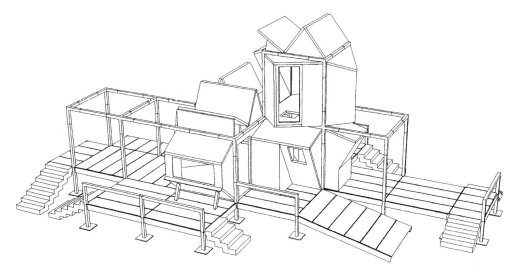

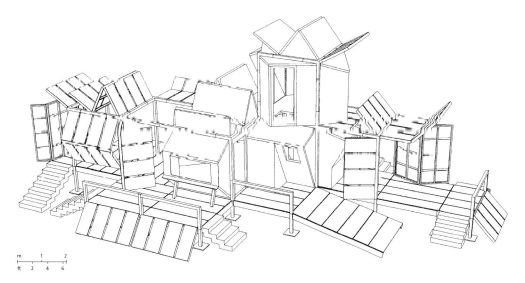

Jantzen has been described as being 20 or 30 years ahead of his time, an epithet also applied to the likes of Buckminster Fuller in his day. While we won't all be living in M-Houses, one can see the attraction of an affordable, sustainable and stylized twenty-first-century cabin that could be trucked in to rural settings with minimal impact on the surroundings and simply lifted away again when its purpose is served.

1 Quoted by Ali Watkinson in her article 'Panel Game', *World of Interiors*, December 2002

CASA DE BLAS
ALBERTO CAMPO BAEZA, Sevilla la Nueva, Madrid, Spain 2000

Pushed into the crest of a hill not far from Madrid, with views of the Sierra de la Almenara, Casa de Blas is an exercise in contrasts. A solid concrete box appears to be partly submerged into the earth, while on top of it sits a glass pavilion forming a viewing platform open to the landscape. Together, these two boxes combine to form a potent new country house.

I wanted to create a belvedere, a place to watch the landscape, which is fascinating, with a magnificent horizon. It's a small acropolis where you can watch, admire, listen to music or be in silence. The owner always says that he asked me for a house for listening to music but I gave him a house to listen to the silence.

So says Alberto Campo Baeza of his creation Casa de Blas, which is perched on a partially wooded, north-facing hillside 20 minutes drive south-east of Madrid. The house is a deceptively simple structure, stripped down to a small collection of essential elements. It is indeed a belvedere, but the word belies the complexity of thought contained within this abstract, geometric game of contrasts. A box-like Miesian glass pavilion, with a steel canopy projecting beyond the line of the frameless windows, sits on top of a larger concrete box, a rectangle pushed lengthways into the top of the hillside, which partly submerges this grey mass within the earth.

left From a distance the house looks little like a house at all – more like an obscure platform or stage – with none of the domestic detailing usually associated with a country home.

right The pavilion has a purposeful transparency, allowing the eye to pass right through the space. The concrete base unit, meanwhile, appears to sink into the earth.

Here we have a floating, transparent, exposed structure above a solid, grounded block or podium speaking weight and mass, sinking downward as though gravity were doing its best to bring the building to heel. A lack of domestic detail and clutter, including gutters and drains, reduces these two forms to pure expressions. The top of the concrete platform is punctured only by a swimming pool at one end and a sunken stairway cut into the floor of the glass pavilion, unencumbered by balustrading or rails. The glass pavilion – within the outline of a canopy supported by eight white columns sitting neatly on the concrete – allows the eye to wander at will, untroubled, with the landscape sweeping in and through the space.

This juxtaposition of ideas of solidity and transparency, gravity and light, mass and motion, enclosure and exposure, lies at the heart of Campo Baeza's work. Its characteristic emphasis on minimalism – or 'essentiality' – does away with distraction and superfluity, concentrating on the dynamic beauty of the space. There are echoes of the De Blas house, for instance, in his Centre for Innovative Technologies at Inca, Majorca. Here, a more complex triangular, limestone-finished,

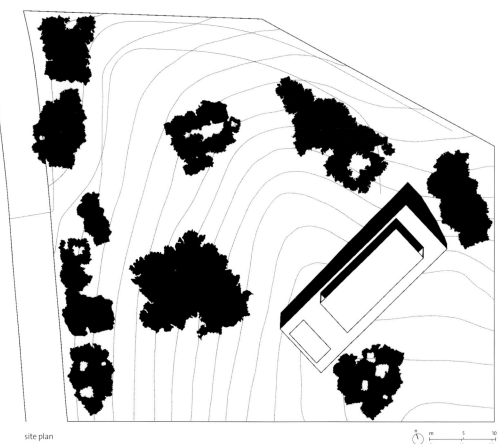

site plan

left The pool is simply recessed into the concrete surface of the base unit, becoming a pure incision in the superstructure. The water and pavilion glass form a thematic alliance.

right The staircase down from the pavilion into the main house is also a simple cut, allowing the pavilion to become almost invisible. Weather and elements appear to pass through.

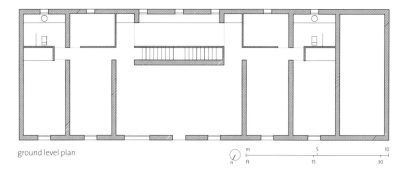

pavilion level plan

ground level plan

elevation

front elevation

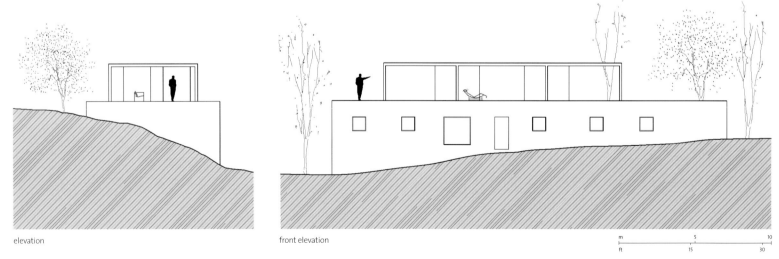

| m | | 5 | | 10 |
| ft | | 15 | | 30 |

concrete-slab building is topped by a triangular glass pavilion, with a similar canopy effect, bordering a rooftop courtyard paved in marble and inset with a sequence of orange trees. Again, we have this striking sense of separation between the solid, grounded base structure and the floating box or belvedere, although acted out on a much larger scale.

Yet the design of the De Blas house was also a very specific response to the site, landscape and the demands of the owner. The pavilion, says Baeza, became a hut for appreciating the countryside, sitting on top of a cave or refuge, reaching down into the hillside. The site itself was somewhat difficult, and rough and ready, with a heavily shifting topography, but the views are sublime. The concrete walls were formed by pouring concrete into wooden moulds, leaving purposeful marks and impressions, which give the building texture and character. These impressions, including wood-grain patterns, are reminiscent of fossilized stone and lend this part of the building an organic quality, which is reinforced by the raw nature of the grounds and the sea of pebbles immediately surrounding the outline of the house.

The concrete section of the house is punctured by a sequence of windows to the front, including one large picture window, as well as the front door. The rear of the building, partly submerged, has a more regular sequence of modest openings. The floor plan is relatively simple, with a large living room and

kitchen at the centre and bathrooms and bedrooms toward the ends of the building, as well as a gym, study and a plant room situated below the pool; most other service areas are pushed to the rear. Here again, detailing is pared down, with whitewashed walls and ceilings and stone floors. The whole fits in with Baeza's axiom of 'achieving everything with almost nothing, more with less'.

And finally, one is drawn back to the pavilion and the idea of the belvedere – a building dedicated to the contemplation and appreciation of the views that inspired its creation. Like the landscape beyond, the house has a feeling of rawness combined with beauty: 'the intelligent kind of beauty that emanates from constructed ideas'.[1] It is a home that is certainly out of the ordinary – stripped down and almost monastic – but one that has a resonance born of a unique and candid response to the countryside.

[1] Quoted by Antonio Pizza in *Alberto Campo Baeza: Works & Projects*, Editorial Gustavo Gili, 1999

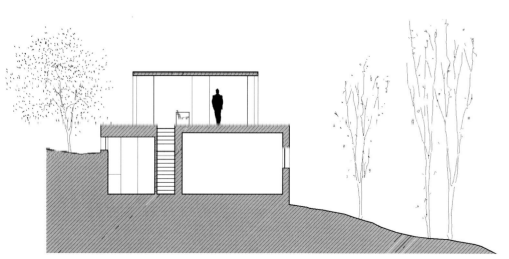

elevation

NAKED HOUSE
SHIGERU BAN, Kawagoe, Saitama, Japan 2000

above The shadows of the trees pass through the building's translucent walls, shifting during the course of the day. Hinged panels around the doorway create a degree of control over the flow of light.

Inspired by the greenhouses and agricultural sheds within this rural location not far from Tokyo, Shigeru Ban has created a luminescent, ethereal family home bordering the paddy fields. Within the large, loft-like interior of the Naked House, space is treated as a fluid and flexible commodity, with four mobile sleeping units that can be pushed and pulled around the building at will.

Shigeru Ban's highly innovative, experimental houses are born from the fortuitous coincidence of the architect's own design agenda with the needs and aspirations of a client with imagination and a spirit of adventure. With the Naked House – one of Ban's latest and most accomplished exercises in space and structure, spliced with an explorer's approach to

materials and building tools – the architect had a client who wanted a flexible, communal home for three generations. The client and his wife have two children (and a dog) as well as the owner's mother living with them. They asked for a modestly budgeted home that 'provides the least privacy so that the family members are not secluded from one another, a house that gives everyone the freedom to have individual activities in a shared atmosphere, in the middle of a unified family'.[1] It was just the kind of brief to fire the architect's thinking.

The Naked House was conceived as essentially one, large, double-height space, with the simple volume of a warehouse or agricultural shed, with a curved wooden roof. The appearance and form of the building were influenced by the greenhouses dotted

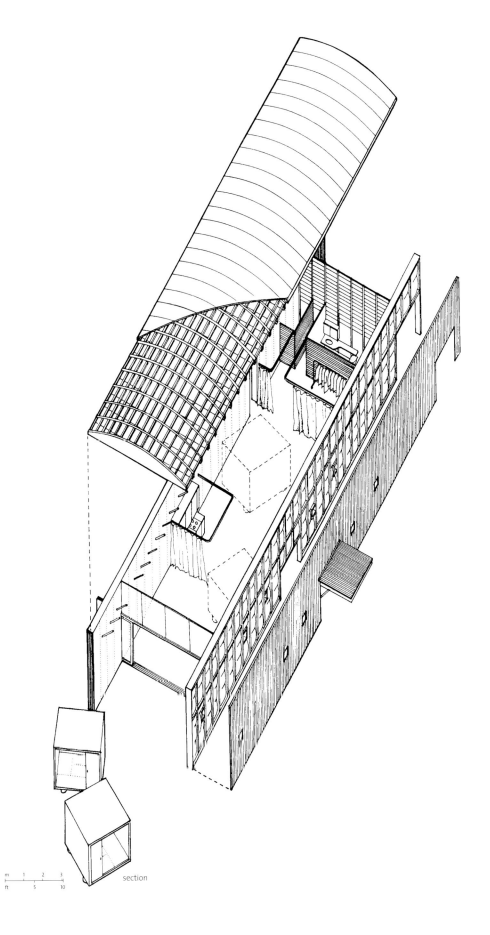

above From inside, the walls retain a pearlescent quality, similar to traditional Japanese rice paper *shoji* screens. Small windows frame aspects of the views across the paddy fields.

section

m 1 2 3
ft   5   10

left The bathroom is one of the very few fully enclosed spaces in the house, situated to one end of the building. The curtain divides an area for bathing from the rest of the room.

right Illuminated at dusk, the house resembles a huge paper lantern. The shape of the building was partly inspired by the greenhouses in this rural area surrounded by fields.

around the rural site of the house, which is bordered by paddy fields with the Shingashi River to one side. The building's translucent walls echo these familiar structures, as well as evoking the pearlescent quality of traditional Japanese *shoji* screens.

The latest in a line of case study houses that experiment with new uses – structural or enveloping – of materials such as paper tubes, curtain fabrics, timber and polycarbonates, the Naked House (or 'Case Study 10') has an unusual skin, 38 centimetres (15 inches) thick made up of three distinct layers attached to a timber frame. The epidermis is made of polycarbonate sheeting, followed by an insulating layer of white polyethylene 'noodles', more commonly used for wrapping and shipping fruit. These were painstakingly fireproofed by Ban's own staff, bagged up and stapled to the supporting timbers. A third, internal, membrane is made of nylon and is attached to the stud frame by strips of Velcro so that it can easily be removed for cleaning. All of these materials share the required semi-transparency, allowing light to pass through the walls of the house so that at night it is illuminated like a vast paper lantern.

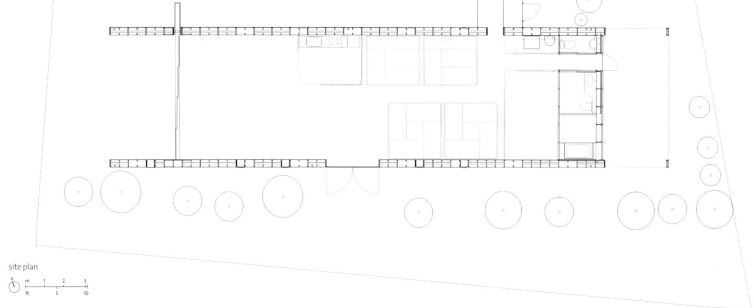

site plan

n
m   1   2   3
ft   5   10

Shitomido panels, hinged at the top, open to reveal double glass doors at the centre of the façade. One end of the building is effectively open ended, with sheet glazing leading to a small terrace. At the other end of this luminous box there is an enclosed bathroom and – beyond the partition wall – a carport, subsumed within the overall structure. Storage and utility areas neighbouring the bathroom – as well as a galley kitchen standing to the rear wall of the open-plan house – can be easily disguised with tracked curtains that surround them, reminiscent of Ban's Curtain Wall house, where curtains formed a delicate outer wrap beyond a layer of glazing.

Within the overall expanse of the Naked House sit four independent, freewheeling mobile units made of paper honeycomb panels on timber frames fixed on castors. These form a quartet of simple *tatami*-matted sleeping blocks that can be moved around the holding space and 'docked' in various positions, as well as linked to one another to form larger modules. The children's bedrooms, which have play areas incorporated on their roofs, can even be moved out onto the terrace. These units are little more than bare spaces, with room enough for futons and little else; clothes and other bits and pieces belong in the dedicated storage space, with

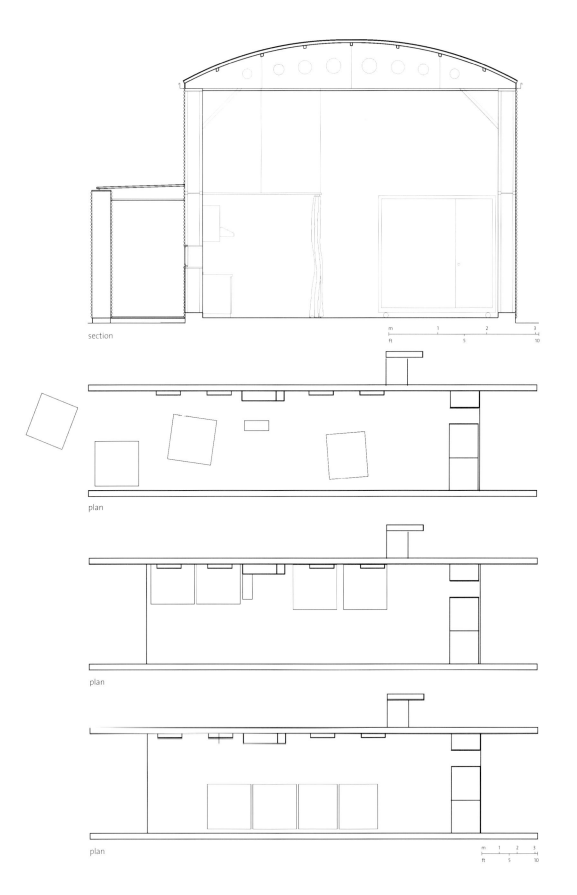

section

plan

plan

plan

hanging space on mobile racks. Removable sliding doors to the sides of the four units offer some sense of privacy.

The Naked House, then, is diaphanous, fluid and communal. It is also minimal, yet ties in with the neat flexibility of traditional Japanese homes, where sliding panels and screens – rather than mobile boxes and curtains – could alter the proportions and function of a space. Once again, Ban's work appears to marry such elements of updated Japanese traditionalism with a spirit of experimentation and a Modernist outlook.

The Naked House is also tied in to its surroundings and the flat, farmland scenery. Small windows in the floating structure frame views, the glazed wall and terrace to one end of the house offering connections with the exterior and the river and fields. But the translucence of the building admits not only patterns of light reflecting the shifts of day and season, but a hazy sense of the world beyond the confines of the house. The nakedness of the building opens it up, in some respects, to the landscape beyond, with nearby trees becoming shadows on the wall as well as sundial clocks.

1 Quoted by Shigeru Ban, briefing notes on the Naked House

VISITING ARTISTS' HOUSE
JIM JENNINGS, Geyserville, California, USA 2003

left The approach to the house enhances a sense of mystery. The terrace suggests nothing of the drama to come as you travel down a choice of two staircases running parallel to the retaining walls.

right The patterns in the vast concrete retaining walls are by artist David Rabinowitch. They dissolve further the lines that separate the idea of house from the theme of land art.

Carved into a Californian hillside at a ranch turned sculpture park, Jim Jennings' Visiting Artists' House is both architectural and sculptural, artificial and organic. With its pair of glass pavilions set between two vast concrete retaining walls cut into the ground, this is a house that uses the idea of submergence to integrate itself into the landscape and frame key vistas.

There is a sense of mystery to Jim Jennings' Visiting Artists' House. Slicing through a hillside crest and partly subsumed by the knoll itself, the purpose and intent of the building initially seem unclear. Set within the grounds of a private sculpture park, the two vast concrete retaining walls, over 60 metres (200 feet) long, which enshrine and protect the house, might be mistaken for another piece of large-scale land art, particularly as the walls are etched with sinuous patterns, carved into the cement surface by New York artist David Rabinowitch. The approach to the house adds to the enigma. You enter

from a raised terrace at the crest of the hill – among the oak trees – where you are met by a series of apparently low-slung walls, with a dual staircase running parallel to the line of the key concrete retaining bastions. Only when you step down the staircase and through a doorway into the heart of the Artists' House do you begin to realize what this space is all about.

This heartland is, in fact, a central courtyard. To either side are two glass pavilions, which connect to and rely upon the retaining walls for support. Each pavilion has an element of transparency, allowing views right through the peripheries, but has a central core containing a bathroom, kitchenette and bedroom, while a fireplace forms a focus for a living room. Each pavilion, then, is fully independent, with the shared, communal element of the courtyard heart plus additional terraces to either end of the overall structure, one framing a view of a nearby lake and the other a vista leading to a large Robert Stackhouse sculpture. Jennings says of the building:

left Seen from some perspectives, the retaining walls offer no suggestion of the house within. The walls appear to emerge from the hillside like the entranceway to a tunnel.

below The central courtyard, with the access point from the entry stairway to the left, is shared by both pavilions, contained within and toward either end of the overall structure.

site plan

I suppose one could say that the house exists both as architecture and as sculpture. The house was designed as architecture but embodies sculptural ideas. I was very interested in the idea of submergence and part of the impulse to dig the building into the ground was to create mystery. I have had architects look at the model and ask, 'How does it work? Where is the light?' It is deceptively simple.

The house was commissioned by Steve Oliver, who has a construction company and a Sonoma county ranch, which has become the focus of his interest in contemporary art and sculpture. Oliver and his wife Nancy have commissioned a number of sculptures for the ranch from artists such as Bruce Nauman, Richard Serra and Ellen Driscoll. They wanted a guest lodge that visiting artists and friends could use, but they did not want it to be overly intrusive or to threaten the privacy of their main residence nearby.

The idea of submergence seems the perfect solution. Indeed, despite the intrinsic artificiality of the materials used – essentially the poured concrete walls and the glass dividers – the house assumes an organic quality by virtue of its partial immersion in the soil and the landscape. 'I also believe that the Visiting Artists' House is "organic" in the Wrightian sense,' says Jennings, 'meaning that its form and spaces grew out of the site and a conceptual response to the site.'

The theme of landscaping is one that has produced some powerful structures with an intrinsically sensitive and empathetic relationship with the countryside, such as Future Systems' House in Wales (see page 8) – reduced to a bank of glazing peeking out of the hillside and looking out to sea – or Gustav Peichl's beautiful Austrian satellite tracking station, where most of the structures are buried

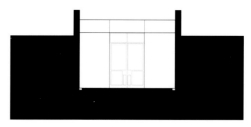

section

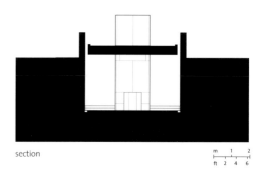

section

m 1   2
ft 2 4 6

left The pavilions are simple structures, largely open plan with a central core holding fireplace, kitchenette and shower room and separating living room to one side and bathroom to the other.

right A framed view from one of the two pavilions out to the sculpture park. As well as the communal one, each pavilion has its own terrace and secondary entrance at the ends of the building.

long section

elevation

m 1 2 3
ft 5 10

underground. The same is true of Hans-Joerg Ruch's Electrical Substation in Albanatscha, Switzerland, which reduces a highly functional and potentially highly intrusive structure to little more than a monolithic stone-clad plinth slipping out of a hillside.

The conceptual nature of this building is enriched by its relationship not only to the land, but also to other pieces of art in the park. The retaining walls, for instance, are not quite parallel but converge slightly, helping to direct the building and the eye to Robert Stackhouse's 30-metre- (100-foot-) long artwork to the east.

The Visiting Artists' House inhabits a theoretical area where art meets Modernist architecture and architecture meets engineering. Its impact on the site is both bold and minimal, adding to the enigmatic nature of the building. Many new country houses have played with submergence, pushing and nudging themselves into existing topographies, but few to such glorious and cohesive effect.

WYE RIVER HOUSE
BELLEMO & CAT, Wye River, Victoria, Australia 2003

Looking like an airship surreally anchored to a hillside among the undulating coastal woodlands of south-west Victoria, Bellemo & Cat's own country escape is a highly inventive structure that nestles into the landscape. Part building, part sculptural expression, it also has the organic, carapace-like nature of a cocoon, chrysalis or animal shell, curled up to protect itself from the elements.

Bellemo & Cat are an unusual practice, even in a country with as vibrant and innovative an architectural scene as Australia. Michael Bellemo is an architect, Cat Macleod an artist and sculptor. They work and collaborate together as designers, artists and architects with a mixed workload of public art and architectural commissions, largely residential, including houses and housing, conversions and extensions. Their work, then, treads that famous overlap where art and architecture combine and tease one another until it is hard to tell which is which.

This is certainly true of their own rural retreat, which provides a much-needed alternative to working and living in the heart of Melbourne. In the words of the architects:

It is as much an artistic expression as a house, and in the course of building it evolved in the way a sculpture might. But it was also a pragmatic response to the need to escape from the hustle and bustle of the city where we were living in a large building with nightclubs beneath us and across the road. We felt a need for a place to retreat to, a nest, a cocoon to grow in.

The spot they chose to nest in was both beautiful and rugged. Two hours drive from Melbourne, Wye River is a place where folding, tree-lined hills meet the ocean. The hillside site for the new house was steep and the climate sometimes harsh, although the trees provide a good deal of shade. The house, then, needed to provide a secure shelter, but also create some sense of connection with the dramatic surroundings.

Bellemo and Macleod came up with the idea of an egg-shaped pebble, a cocoon, or – as the locals call it –'the footy'. This was a form that met the need for a lightweight structure that could be raised off the ground and sit deftly within the fragile, sloping site, as well as being well insulated, wrapped and protected. It was also a promising sculptural form, within which contrasts could be created between the more rectangular elements of the main living space

right The house perches on the edge of a hillside slope, anchored in place by steel supports. The steel shingle skin gives the appearance of an organic, animal shell.

– essentially a box within an egg – and curvilinear sections to the tip of the ovoid shell, where the master bedroom is located.

In designing and building the house, they drew upon the kind of craftsmanship and engineering usually applied to boat building and aircraft engineering, while the spatial qualities of the cocoon mirror the kind of ingenuity shown in caravans and RVs – or airships. A rectangular structure was built first, to hold the main living and utility areas. A series of plywood ribs were added to the rectangle to begin creating the enveloping cocoon, and hardwood battens were then attached to these ribs. This

formed a frame over which steel shingles were fixed to form a hard, protective skin or shell, firm enough to add to the overall structural integrity of the house.

Six steel legs anchor the house to its hillside spot and a boat-like gangplank leads to the entrance to the rear, where a flat area forms a parking spot and the house is largely closed off. To the other side, looking out, down and across the trees, a viewing platform or balcony was welded on, accessed by a series of sliding glass doors. This balcony helps open the house up to the landscape and provides a key source of light for the main living space. A galley kitchen runs down the opposite side of this open-plan living area, while a

bathroom and utility room lie beyond a 'bulkhead', with bedrooms in the nose cone. The children's bedrooms use bunk beds to maximize space.

The house, then, assumes an organic, low-key, but sculpted and artful presence in the bush. It settles itself into the site, opening its side to the landscape, while the shell ties itself by association to the natural world. 'There is a fascination in the tension between the perfect symmetry of the structure and the crinkled carapace or rippled skin that takes on the character of the animals of the bush', say Bellemo & Cat.

The Wye River House becomes a land-sensitive resort cabin, drawing on a melange of influences and ideas. Like Michael Jantzen's M-House (see pages 168–173), it could well be seen as a prototypical version of a lightweight, flexible vacation home. But, again like the M-House, it is an individual expression and a particular way of living, one that has the elegant beauty of a crafted object placed in the gallery of the land.

left The master bedroom sits in the 'nose cone' of the house. The rounded, circular nature of the space creates a contrast to the more regular appearance of the living room.

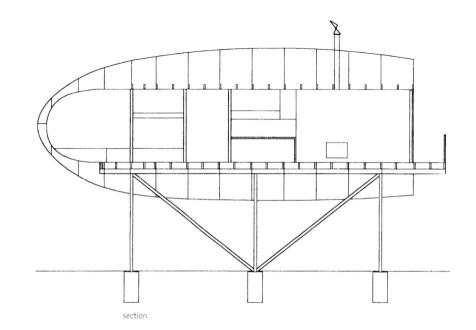

section

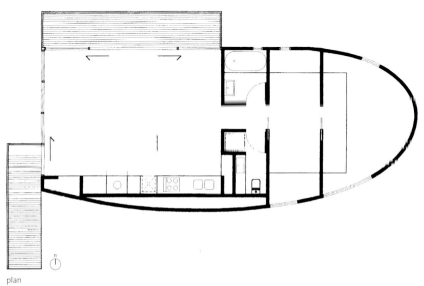

plan

THE BUTTERFLY HOUSE
LAURIE CHETWOOD, Dunsfold, Surrey, UK 2003

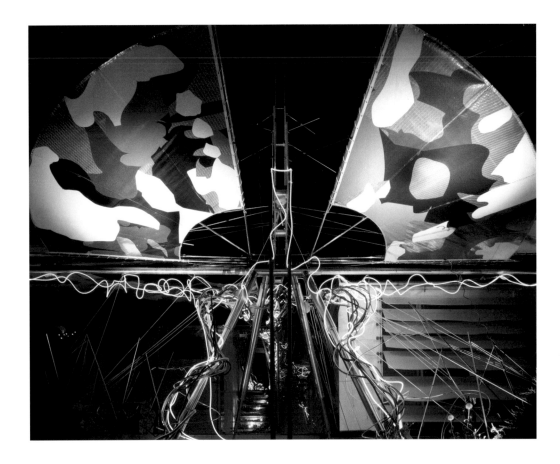

A personal statement and a laboratory for
experimenting with form and materials, Laurie
Chetwood's Butterfly House takes its zoomorphic
inspiration from the natural world and surrounding
landscape. A metaphorical exploration of a
butterfly's lifecycle, complete with a winged canopy,
it is a light-hearted but wholly inventive
reinterpretation of the rural retreat.

The Butterfly House has burst out of the chrysalis
shell of an older, more traditional building. Laurie
Chetwood and his family were initially drawn to this
quiet, rural 1.2-hectare (three-acre) site on a south-
facing slope on the Surrey/Sussex border by the
landscape and the views. But the original house was
uninspiring: a small cedar-framed and -clad two-
bedroomed Canadian kit house that had been shown
at the Ideal Home Show of 1930, stored and then
erected on site in 1948 as a vacation home. Having

stood empty for the best part of two decades, the
house was in poor condition and lacked insulation
and other essentials. Having bought the site in 1993,
Chetwood hoped he might be able to remove the
house and replace it with something different, but
planning restrictions meant he had to think again.

As Chetwood worked on securing the house
and making it habitable, he noticed that the area
was rich with butterflies, attracted by the planting
around the house – lavender, buddleia and so on.
The butterflies started him thinking and he
commissioned an ecological study, which suggested
that the family had wandered into an ideal butterfly
breeding ground.

The architect's practice, Chetwood Associates, is
better known for its large-scale developments, hotels
and supermarkets than for individual houses. But
Chetwood has a long-held passion for zoomorphic,
fluid forms and curvilinear architecture that adopts

lessons and ideas from the natural world. His award-winning supermarket on the Greenwich Peninsula, for instance, is enriched by an armadillo-like shell-roof with long stripes of embedded glazing.

With his own house, he had the good fortune to be able to take these interests to an extreme, treating the dramatic reinvention of the old 1930s building into futuristic, zoomorphic Butterfly House as part indulgence, part experiment. He looked at a variety of materials, forms and structures, some of which the practice might be able to develop and explore elsewhere on a more commercial, client-led basis. In Chetwood's own words:

Within nature form follows function so well and rather better than within Modernist architecture. It is an area that I'm passionate about. If you give me a pencil I will always start to draw in curves rather than straight lines. And I did a lot of artwork when I was younger, in the 1970s, and there was so much organic, zoomorphic design around at the time from Yes *album covers to* Star Wars. *It was almost inbred as we grew up and now has a tendency to come out in our work.*

The design of the Butterfly House took some years to evolve – to some extent it is still evolving – as Chetwood played with ideas and talked to planners. Some initial thoughts were dismissed; others were developed and redeveloped. Given the totally bespoke nature of the house, many elements were built twice over. The result is an extraordinary and highly complex building filled with imaginative

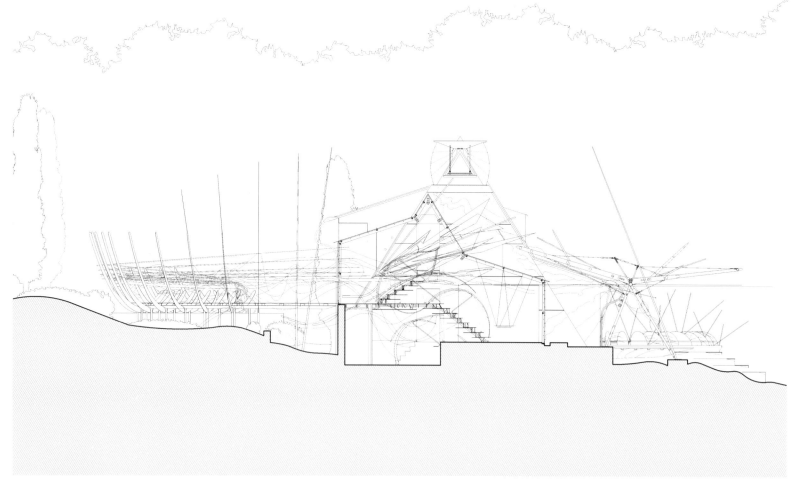

elevation

games and eco-awareness, while that old 1930s building has been subsumed under many layers of artistry and eccentricity.

The building, then, has become an extended metaphor for the lifecycle of the butterfly. A curving steel-ribbed walkway that takes you into a raised-level entrance at the back of the house was inspired by the form of a chrysalis. Internally, the house is intended to suggest the emergence of the butterfly, with the convoluted stairway and elements of the main living spaces suggesting the unfolding wings. Dominating the façade and providing summer shelter for the new conservatory and terrace is an arrangement of unfolding butterfly wings, forming a protective canopy.

left The wings are just one part of the metaphorical layering applied to the house – though they are also the most dramatic. They become a focal point for the outward appearance of the house.

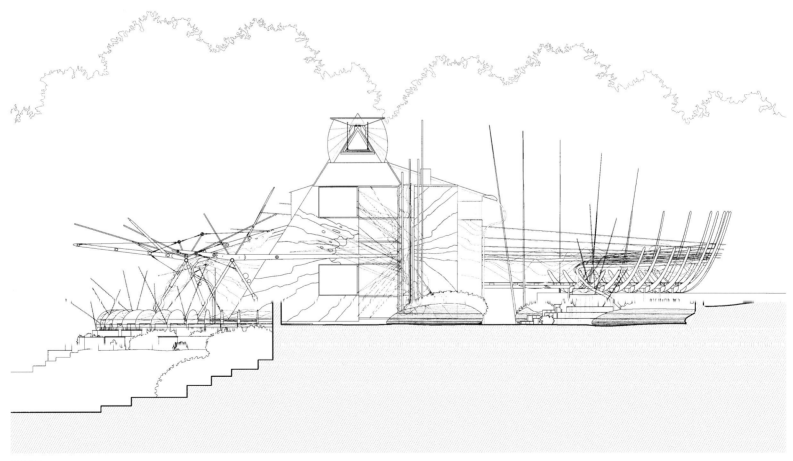

elevation

right A long, curving
suspended walkway
reaches round the rear of
the house and arrives at a
raised entrance hallway.
The zoomorphic form of
the structure was inspired
by a chrysalis.

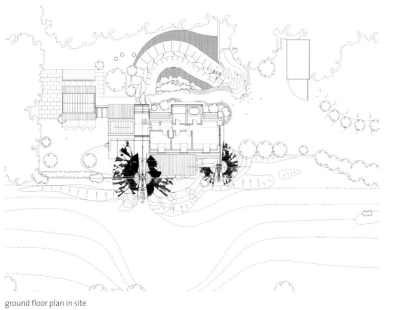

ground floor plan in site

first floor plan in site

Within this metaphorical framework sit many other thoughts and experiments, again largely inspired by the zoomorphic theme, from an accentuated barrel chimney coated in copper to suspended tables and benches in layers of Perspex. On the one hand there is the poetic nature of the butterfly metaphor, but on the other an extreme, sci-fi-inspired, postmodern, Pompidou-like emphasis on exposed workings, pipework and wiring.

Ultimately, the Butterfly House is a personal venture, as well as a unique family house and country home, related closely to its surroundings. It is also a laboratory experiment, which has already led to commissions for other one-off houses, including a project in the Andes. This combination of personality and zoomorphic experiment places the building in a loose tradition of individual concept houses by the likes of Eugene Tsui, whose Reyes House was inspired by a dragonfly; Herb Greene, whose Oklahoma Prairie House was modelled on the form of a buffalo; and Michael Reynolds, whose Nautilus Earthship is based on a seashell form. Each is eccentric and distinct, but also provocative and a testing ground for ideas and innovations that filter into the broader architectural milieu and spark new thinking and new approaches.

INDEX

Figures in *italics* refer to captions; those in **bold** to main entries

PROJECT DETAILS

Alex + Mase House
Architect Jesus Irisarri & Guadalupe Pinera

Berman House
Architect Harry Seidler & Associates

Büchel House
Architect Baumschlager & Eberle
Planning B&E GmbH Lochau
Client Fam. Büchel

Butterfly House, The
Architect Laurie Chetwood, Chetwood Associates, London
Project Team Laurie Chetwood, Roz Marzano, Stuart Cross, Carlos Dublanc,
Christoph Recktenwald Edmund

Casa, La
Architect Elizabeth Wright Ingraham & Associates
Structural Engineers Howard C Dutzi & Associates, Inc., Colorado Springs
Mechanical Engineers Merritt Engineering Inc., Colorado Springs
Landscape Architect Gernot Heinrichsdorff, A.S.L.A., Colorado Springs
Electrical Consultants Plant Engineering Consultants, Colorado Springs
Specification Consultants Specification Consultants, Terry Strong, Colorado Springs
Sculpture in Niche Ivan Kosta, Sculptor
Decorative Tiles Lou Wynne, Ceramist
General Contractor Mahler-Gambucci Construction, Inc., Colorado Springs

Casa de Blas
Architect Alberto Campo Baeza
Collaborator Raúl del Valle
Client Francisco De Blas
Structural Engineer Maria Concepción Pérez Gutiérrez
Management Francisco Melchor
Main Contractor Juan Sáinz

Casa Tagomago
Architect Carlos Ferrater
Collaborator Joan Guibernau

Cavegn House
Architect Ivan Cavegn
Project Team Ivan Cavegn Architekturbüro, Vaduz, Liechtenstein
Structural Engineer Pius Mündle Ingenieurbüro, Mauren, Liechtenstein

Colorado House
Architect Architecture Research Office
Staff John Quale (project architect), Scott Abrahams, Monica Rivera, Martha Skinner, Kim Yao,
Thomas Jenkinson, Matt Azen, Jiayur Hsu, Mikael Hoilund

House on Mount Fuji
Architect Satoshi Okada Architects
Project Manager Lisa Tomiyama, Eisuke Aida
Structural Engineer Kenta Masaki

Jacob's Ladder
Architect Niall McLaughlin
Clients David and Shelley Grey

Keenan Towerhouse
Architect Marlon Blackwell, Arkansas
Project Team Marlon Blackwell, Meryati Johari-Blackwell, Dianne Meek, Phil Hatfield
Owner James Keenan
Contractors Razorback Ironworks + Pizzini + Don Lourie, Arkansas
Engineers Joe Looney, Structural Engineer, Arkansas

M-House
Architect Michael Jantzen
Engineers Advanced Structures Inc., Los Angeles

Marte Single Family House
Architect Marte & Marte
Project Team Stefan Marte, Bernhard Marte, Michelangelo Zaffignani, Konrad Klostermann,
Robert Zimmermann
Client Stefan and Margot Marte
Main Contractor Concrete Works Wilhelm + Mayer, Götzis
Structural Engineer M+G Ingenieure in Feldkirch

Moledo House
Architect Eduardo Souto de Moura
Collaborators Manuela Lara, Pedro Reis, Nuno Rodrigues Pereira
Client António Reis
Structural Consultants José Adriano Cardoso

Mountain Guest House
Architect Mack Scogin Merrill Elam
Project Team Mack Scogin, Merrill Elam, David Yocum, Penn Ruderman, Denise Dumais
Builder Winfred & Warren McKay, Winfred McKay Construction, Dillard, Georgia
Structural Engineer Palmer Engineering, Tucker, Georgia: Chris DeBlois, Bianca Roberts
Landscape Designers Marchant Martin
Lighting Designers Ramón Noya, Ramón Luminance Design, Atlanta, Georgia

Naked House
Architect Shigeru Ban
Project Team Shigeru Ban, Mamiko Ishida, Anne Scheou
General Contractors Misawaya Kensetsu
Structural Engineers Hoshino Architect & Engineer – Shuichi Hoshino, Takashige Suzuki

Oberwalder/Kutscha House
Architect Büro Ko a la
Project team Ko a la
Client Robert Kutscha, Veronika Oberwalder
Main Contractor SB Massivbau
Structural Engineer Gerhard Baumkirchner

Red House
Architect Jarmund/Vigsnæs Architects AS Architects MNAL (Einar Jarmund & Håkon Vigsnæs)
Assisted by Roar Lund-Johnsen
Contractor Ing. Gunnar Johnansson AS
Interiors Jarmund/Vigsnæs Architects AS Architects MNAL
Consultant Structural: Ing. Walter Jacobsen

Rogers Residence
Architect Westwork Architects
Builder's Name Lewton Construction
Client Corinne L. Shefner-Rogers and Everett M. Rogers

Sheep Farm House
Architect Denton Corker Marshall Pty Ltd
Contractor Multiplex Constructions Pty Ltd
Engineers Bonacci Winward Pty Ltd
Landscape Architects Denton Corker Marshall Pty Ltd

Single Family House
Architect Brückner & Brückner Architekten
Planning Project Management Brückner & Brückner Architekten, Tirschenreuth (Christian Brückner & Peter Brückner)
Project Team Robert Reith, Wolfgang Herrmann
Structural Engineers Brückner & Brückner Ingenieure Tirschenreuth Dipl.-Ing Klaus-Peter Brückner
Building Services Engineers Ingenieurbüro Reicholt Kemnath Dipl.-Ing. Manfred Reicholt

Summer Residence
Architect Henning Larsen
Project Team Henning Larsen, Peer Teglgaard Jeppesen (project manager), Anders Park, Claus Simonsen
Client Gallery owner Mikhael Andersen
Main Contractor Langelinie Byg ApS
Structural Engineer Anders Christensen

Sutterlüty House
Architect Dietrich Untertrifäller Architekten, Bregenz, Austria
Project Manager Walter Felder
Client Fred Sutterlüty
Engineers Markus Flatz, Bregenz

Visiting Artists' House
Architect Jim Jennings Architecture
Project Team Michael Lin, Cherl Fraser, Troy Schaum, Paul Burgin, Les Taylor, May Fung
Interior Furniture Gary Hutton Design
Landscape Consultant Andrea Cochran
Lighting Consultant Dan Dodt
Consulting Architect Tim Perks
General contractor Oliver & Company

Westlake House
Architect SpacelabUK
Project Team Andrew Budgen & Nathan Lonsdale (SpacelabUK)
Client John & Terri Westlake
Main Contractor Granville Building Company
Structural Engineer Peter Dann Limited

Willimann-Lötscher House
Architect Bearth & Deplazes Architekten AG Valentin Bearth & Andrea Deplazes, Chur Partner, Daniel Ladner
Clients Therese Lötscher & Urban Willimann
Engineer Jürg Buchli, Haldenstein

Wye River House
Architects Bellemo & Cat
Project Team Michael Bellemo, Cat Macleod
Builder Keith A Reid
Structural Engineer Peter Felicetti Pty Ltd

Y House
Architect Steven Holl
Project Architect Erik Langdalen
Project Team Annette Goderbauer, Yoh Hanaoka, Brad Kelley, Justin Korhammer, Jennifer Lee, Chris McVoy
Architect on Site Peter Liaunig
Structural Engineers Robert Silman Associates PC
Lighting Consultant L'Observatoire International

Yomiuri Guest House
Architect Atelier Hitoshi Abe
Structural Engineer TIS & Partners
Mechanical Engineer Sogo Consultants
Constructor Sugawara Construction
Other Consultants Sano Consultants

BIBLIOGRAPHY

Emilio Ambasz et al, *Shigeru Ban*, Laurence King, 2001.

Paco Asensio, *Mountain Houses*, Loft Publications/HBI, 2000.

Alejandro Bahamon, *Mini Houses*, HBI, 2003.

Kenneth Baker (Ed.), *The Faber Book of Landscape Poetry*, Faber & Faber, 2000.

Haig Beck et al, *Denton Corker Marshall: Rule Playing and the Ratbag Element*, Birkhäuser, 2000.

Haig Beck et al, *10x10*, Phaidon, 2000.

Aaron Betsky, *Landscrapers: Building With Land*, Thames & Hudson, 2002.

Werner Blaser, *Eduardo Souto de Moura: Stone Element*, Birkhäuser, 2003.

Bruce Brooks Pfeiffer, *Frank Lloyd Wright*, Taschen, 2000.

René Burn, *Luis Barragán*, Phaidon, 2000.

Jessica Cargill Thompson, *40 Architects Under 40*, Taschen, 2000.

Stephen Cassell & Adam Yarinsky, *ARO: Architecture Research Office*, Graham Foundation/Princeton Architectural Press, 2002.

Aurora Cuito, *Country Modern*, Loft Publications/HBI, 2001.

David Dernie, *New Stone Architecture*, Laurence King, 2003.

Stephen Dobney (Ed.), *Harry Seidler: Selected and Current Works*, Images, 1997.

Carlos Ferrater, *Carlos Ferrater*, Phaidon, 2002.

Kenneth Frampton, *Steven Holl Architect*, Electa, 2002.

Francesco Garofalo, *Steven Holl*, Thames & Hudson, 2003.

Jacob & Wilhelm Grimm, *The Complete Illustrated Stories of the Brothers Grimm*, Chancellor Press, 1984.

Jim Jennings, *Jim Jennings Architecture: Ten Projects, Ten Years*, William Stout, 1998.

Philip Jodidio, *Architecture Now!*, Taschen, 2001.

Philip Jodidio, *Architecture Now! Volume Two*, Taschen, 2002.

David Lloyd Jones, *Architecture and the Environment*, Laurence King, 1998.

Matilda McQuaid, *Shigeru Ban*, Phaidon, 2003.

Clare Melhuish, *Modern House 2*, Phaidon, 2000.

Massimo Preziosi (Ed.), *Carlos Ferrater: Works & Projects*, 2002.

Antonio Pizza et al, *Alberto Campo Baeza: Works and Projects*, GG, 1999.

Nicolas Pople, *Experimental Houses*, Laurence King, 2000.

Nicolas Pople, *Small Houses*, Laurence King, 2003.

Vicky Richardson, *New Vernacular Architecture*, Laurence King, 2001.

John Ruskin, *Selected Writings*, Everyman, 1995

James Soane, *New Home*, Conran Octopus, 2003.

Steven Spier & Martin Tschanz, *Swiss Made: New Architecture from Switzerland*, Thames & Hudson, 2003.

Naomi Stungo, *The New Wood Architecture*, Laurence King, 1998.

Deyan Sudjic, *Home: The Twentieth Century House*, Laurence King, 1999.

Henry David Thoreau, *Walden & Civil Disobedience*, Penguin, 1983.

Adrian Tinniswood, *Country Houses from the Air*, Phoenix, 1994.

Liesbeth Waechter-Böhm, *Baumshlager & Eberle: Buildings & Projects, 1996–2002*, Springer Verlag, 2003.

Evelyn Waugh, *Brideshead Revisited*, Penguin, 1962.

John Welsh, *Modern House*, Phaidon, 1995.

Richard Weston, *The House in the Twentieth Century*, Laurence King, 2002.

James Wines, *Green Architecture*, Taschen, 2000.

Walter Zschokke, *Helmut Dietrich & Much Untertrifaller*, Springer Verlag, 2001.

PICTURE CREDITS